Ethnologia Europaea

Journal of European Ethnology

Volume 27:1 1997

MUSEUM TUSCULANUM PRESS · UNIVERSITY OF COPENHAGEN

Printed in Sweden by BTJ Tryck AB, Lund 1997
ISBN 87-7289-464-4
ISSN 0425-4597

This journal is published with the support of Nordic Publication Committee for Humanist Periodicals.

Museum Tusculanum Press
University of Copenhagen
Njalsgade 92
DK-2300 Copenhagen S.

The Functions of Things

Albert Baiburin

Baiburin, Albert 1997: The Functions of Things. – Ethnologia Europaea 27: 3–14.

The following paper deals with the problem of the functions of things in a traditional culture. Based on material on the Eastern Slavs, particularly Russians, it considers a life "scenario" of things by introducing a concept of semiotic status of things. It will be shown that the status is dependent on a context of functioning. Particular attention has been given to informational aspects of things and their functions in ritual context. A distinction is made between the capacity of things to symbolise "one's own" and "alien" concepts, to function as mediators between these two worlds and, on the contrary, to block the communication channel between them.

Albert Baiburin, Dr.Sc. (History), Senior Researcher, Peter the Great Museum of Anthropology and Ethnography (Kunstkammer), Russian Academy of Sciences; Dean, Department of Ethnology, European University at St. Petersburg, 3 Furmanov Street, St. Petersburg 191187, Russia.

The "Birth" of Things

Fundamental peculiarities of the functioning of things in an archaic culture reveal themselves already in the process of their manufacture. Ample evidence, particularly myths of craft origins, points to the fact that, in creating a thing, man in a certain sense repeated those operations that in the Beginning could be performed only by the Creator or Creators of the Universe. Thus, man continued the demiurge-initiated task of world creation, having assumed the challenges of not only replacing natural losses but also further filling-in and embodying the world. In this way the process of creating things entered a cosmological scheme. It is no surprise that the technology of manufacturing things referred to the sphere of sacred knowledge. Specific attributes, faculties and knowledge were ascribed to the specialists (smiths, potters, builders, etc.) in almost all cultures, serving as a basis for their segregation (cf. distinctive castes of craftsmen in Ancient Orient). Among those specific traits one surprisingly stable aspect has engaged our attention: the power and might of the specialists were seen by the rest of the society as falling outside the scope of the craft. Due to their knowledge, they gained the ability of communicating with those powers which might affect people's destiny. We could say that they were attributed with proficiency in a language difficult for others.

Apart from this, the specialists were not only proficient in the specific language, but also controlled the communication channel between the world of man and the world of nature, acting as peculiar mediators. Phenomena related to the outer world are likely to have had, for bearers of an archaic and traditional society, a status other than that which it would have for us today. Whereas we are used to treating them as phenomena and not objects, for an archaic man, rather, they are subjects. The case in point is radically different types of attitude of man toward the world around him. In the first case, the "Me–It" scheme is realised, and the "Me–You" scheme in the other. The attitude of the first type correlates with scientific cognition. The second type of attitude emerges when man can understand another living creature (Frankfort et al. 1967: 5; cf. Averintsev 1977: 40). Strictly speaking, in the latter case there is no generalised relation with the other, no less living creatures than man himself. Such an understanding of the nature of relationships between man and the environment does not necessarily mean a return to the "animistic" and "personalistic" concepts of different sorts. For the man oriented toward a traditional world perception, an "animated" world does not exist, since there cannot be an "inanimate" one in principle (Frankfort et al. 1967: 6). The situation in which the outer world is full of living creatures of another, non-human nature, suggests an understanding, provided there is a dialogue. A constant and extremely emotional dialogue between man and the natural environment presents another trait of traditional culture. This is especially profound in different strategies of the exploration of the outer world. While modern technological thought and production aim at the conquest of the outer world, a tendency was inherent in traditional (and more so, in archaic) culture to collaborate with it, and to adopt its "responses" with the aim of achieving mutually beneficial results (Toporov 1983: 230). This "partnership", the perception of an inseparable connection, the striving to act in unison with and not counter to nature were seen as a pledge of success in every activity.

This attitude toward the natural environment determined peculiarities of the procedure of selecting materials for the manufacture of things. Notions of the categories of the "suitable" and "useful" were quite different from ours. To be suitable a material should meet not only physical but also symbolic requirements (cf. "... the reasons why different societies choose to utilize or reject certain natural products and, if they do utilize them, the modes of employment they choose depend not only upon the intrinsic properties of the products but also on the symbolic values ascribed to them." Lévi-Strauss 1972: 95). To some degree, it is necessary that a material should fit in a universal classification of surrounding phenomena which correlates with such concepts as life, happiness, purity, etc. D.G. Redder (*Kultura* 1976: 247) states that

"in the manner of concepts of high merits of man situated in the centre of the Universe created by God or Gods especially for him, the classification of plants, animals and minerals was made. Good or evil done to the people were recognised as the main characteristic. Certainly, these indicators were frequently of an unreal, magical character. Malachite, for instance, was considered a sacred stone because it has a colour of life (green), and quartz, with its colour reminiscent of a desert, used to be declared profane and rejected."

From this standpoint it is extremely significant that, for example, the reasons why the Bronze Age came earlier than the Iron Age were of not a technical (bronze is more difficult to cast than iron) but of valuational character: bronze is likely to have been widespread in the ritual sphere (Ivanov 1983: 89–90). Numerous examples can be offered of non-use, for practical purposes, of plants, minerals, wood, animal species, etc. simply on the grounds that they were correlated with a negative paradigm of meanings. At the same time, an "individual" approach to the choice of the material for the prospective thing turned out to be essential, in which process the foreground was taken by extra-utilitarian considerations, for each phenomenon had its own particular features as dictated, for example, by a place, coloration, condition and the like. (Cf. "If a larch-tree or a pine tree or an aspen grows up on an ant-hill, [they] make a trough out of it in which livestock are fed: a good offspring may happen. If the tree is too short to make a trough from – [they] break off its branch and stick it in the yard – for good offspring." Vinogradov 1918: 19–20)

Surprisingly detailed classifications of plants and animals in different archaic cultures are well known. Properly speaking, such classifications present one of the results of that dialogue between man and nature mentioned above. It is their characteristics (hierarchical nature, volume, etc.) that allow them to be considered as specific developments of the initial classification which was designated by the myth and ritual of creation. In this connection, we cannot but cite a remark by C. Lévi-Strauss (1973: 9) that all those animals and plants are known to early man not because they are useful. On the contrary, many of these are considered useful due primarily to their already being known, integrated into a unified, global classified complex which helps man orient himself within the environment (Toporov 1982: 29–30). Basic materials for necessities (metals, clay, wood, wool, etc.) possessed a special status: it was these that served as the initial resources for the creation of the world and man himself (cf. Caucasian myths of forging man and the world; making man of clay in the mythologies of Ancient Egypt, the Dogons of Western Sudan, and in Chinese myths; the construction of the world by divine carpenters in Rigveda; the creation of the world by the "weaver", Neit, of Egyptian myths, etc.). The principal participants in the technological process – man (who assumed the functions of God) and the elements (fire, water and air) – duplicate in fact the participants of the cosmological act of creating, causing the world to emerge.

The rules governing the creation of the world formed the basis for primitive technology. The principal schemes of world creation and material production are one and the same: 1) the introduction of space and time indicators: light and darkness, day and night, top and bottom, skies and earth (cf. compulsory space and time limitations in manufacturing things); 2) the selection of material; 3) the transformation of the material with the help of natural agents (water, fire, air); 4) the "animation" of the created. We shall dwell on the latter two.

Scholars of ancient industries (forging, pottery, plaiting, weaving, building, etc.) tend to notice repeatedly the "excessiveness" of the technological processes, i.e. the presence of a multitude of operations that, from the modern point of view, had no impact on the final outcome. Besides, the technical methods themselves had not only technical significance (cf. as an example, taboos on sewing, spinning, scutching flax and warping during the wake: "You will sew grandfathers' eyes", "You will block up the eyes of forefathers", etc.).

These operations derived a name of the "rites accompanying...", for instance, the manufacture of pottery. Not infrequently they were simply ignored as non-obligatory supplements to rational processes. Nevertheless, there are grounds to argue that it is the ritual that gave birth to technology rather than having served as a mere "accompaniment" to it, a wholly useful object resulting from a ritual was thought of as a sequel of the validity of the initial scheme, as a substantiation of its fruitfulness. In other words, the correlation between practical and symbolic aspects of material production was just opposite. Practical suitability of things was determined, among others, by the correspondence of two rituals – creation of the world and manufacture of things.

The point of what preconditioned the choice of the form of things – either their functional purpose or a mythological concept – has not been finally established. It is clear that the form of a thing always corresponded to one of the phenomenal forms known to man from his natural environment. And this correspondence was far from being arbitrary. By giving things, for example, forms of animals, man thus endowed those things with properties and outlines of the animals. The same effect was also achieved through the ornamentation, effigies – all that we refer to as decorative design. In any case, properties of things, including practical ones, are directly dependent on *what* is depicted on them or *what* they depict themselves. That is the reason why the design of things made no allowance for imagination. It was profoundly pragmatic and not facultative as in modern culture. "For an artist of modern differentiated society there are no limitations in choosing motifs for decorating a thing; they can be drawn from cultures of all times and all peoples. The surface of a thing is regarded as freed of any semantic connotation, it is similar to a canvas stretched on a sub-frame. For primitive and traditional craftsmen the "decor" of a thing and the very thing, as well as its purpose, were linked together in a special way. One of the goals of decorating things is to give them a special strength. According to M.-P. Fousche, an Australian boomerang was believed to be capable of hitting the target only if ornamented (Antonova 1984: 49). This notion was widely spread: for example, in the Russian North spinning wheels otherwise ready for use were not used or considered suitable until they were decorated. More precisely, it has to do not with the decorating of things in a common sense, but with endowing them with necessary (as well as practical) properties, with their animating. Only in this event does a thing start to function both as a useful item and as a wholly living phenomenon with strictly individual properties. "Things are endowed with the same property as the humans or natural phenomena – “character”. What the function of a thing is for us, is the manifestation of the thing’s own, inherent features for a man thinking mythologically” (Antonova 1984: 30).

A newly made thing has to pass a test of a sort. It should be noted, that the category of “new” occupied a special place within the system of hierarchical concepts. The ritual value of new things was considerably high. They were incorporated into the structure of many rituals (cf. the role of fresh flour in calendar rites; of new linen in family ones, etc.). As is known, there were specific rituals of making things which were used only when new and exclusively for symbolic purposes (the so called everyday things). At the same time, new things were handled prudently. This can be explained by several reasons. Firstly, until they are put in extensive use (both practically and ritually), new things are to a greater extent part of the sphere of the alien (unexplored) and not the human. Secondly, it is unknown to what extent a newly made thing corresponds with the sacred prototype (not only by appearance but also by inner properties). The procedure and character of the test of new items as exemplified by dwellings are considered elsewhere (Baiburin 1983). It would be appropriate to note one circumstance here: if unsatisfactory practical properties were found, a man would not have been inclined to see the reason for this in the quality of the material or the technical aspect. For him it meant only that the ritual of creating the thing did not correspond with the proto-ritual. The discrepancy was seen first of all in symbolic operations, since it is they that determine practical properties, and not vice versa. Such things with a defective set of properties were not introduced into the world of man. Moreover, they became the focus of powers hostile to man (cf. notions associated with new but abandoned houses).

A satisfactory outcome indicated the emergence of a new thing with the structure of functions we are not accustomed to. Such a thing, apart from practical significance, had a wide spectrum of symbolic functions and presented a model of the world, being probably perceived as a living being with its specific features. That is why the words of E.V. Antonova (1984: 30) seem to be correct: “...from the standpoint of mythological thinking a man-made thing is identical to all the rest of things in the world. It came to the world in the way identical to the one which had led to the emergence of the earth, heavenly bodies, animals and man. Like other things, it was endowed with properties of a living creature. The thing seems to be inseparable from the world, it represents the world itself and not its reflection”. After this brief description of the principal scheme of the “birth” of things we shall proceed to examining the “life” of things and the specifics of their functioning in an archaic society.

“Thing-ness” and “Symbol-ness”

The above discussion of specific features of ancient technology has a direct relationship to the problem of the functioning of things. The integrity of an archaic culture, coupled with the absence of specialised tools to ensure the circulation of information within a society, was responsible for each element of culture being used far more completely, accurately and extensively than in modern society.

The cultural significance and value of an archaic and traditional thing were essentially higher than those of a modern one. Apart from universal practical requirements set up for things in all times, they had to meet extra-utilitarian needs as well. In other words, things were “set in motion” in a practical respect and were used extensively in a game of meaning along with other elements of culture, which, like things, were used not only for their “immediate purpose” but also as signs of social relations. There is a lack here of the specialisation of sign systems, the division into the world of symbols and the world of things which is so typical of contemporary society. Here things are always symbols, just as symbols are things.

As semiotic tools, not only language, myth and ritual are used, but also the utensils, economic and social institutions, kinship systems, dwellings, food, clothing etc. All these cultural symbols share a united and common structure of meanings, due to which fact chains of various correspondences are possible, for example: utensil – landscape element – bodily part – unit of social structure – time of year, etc. Such a surprising unity of substantially different phenomena in the archaic perception of the world made it possible for scholars to claim the idea that an archaic culture represents an integrated semiotic system, with each of its elements correlated with all other elements, and all of them "participating in a common all-inclusive metaphor" (Segal 1986: 39).

The unity of the symbolic and practical which is inherent in all man-made or man-used things, and their principal ambivalence, have given rise to the formulation of the notion of the semiotic status of things which is necessary, in our opinion, for a more adequate description of the functioning of things in cultures of various types (Baiburin 1981: 215–226). The fact is that the widespread scholarly division of phenomena of reality into the world of facts and the world of symbols (Lotman 1970: 14) is rather conventional, as there are always intermediate objects. To those elements of "material culture" relate. When entering into a semiotic system (for instance, into a ritual), they function as symbols, when falling out – as things.

In other words, such phenomena may potentially be used both as things and symbols. Depending on what properties are actualised ("thing-ness" or "symbol-ness"), they gain one or another semiotic status, i.e. occupy a certain position on the scale of the semioticity of phenomena, artificially introduced by man. Thus, the semiotic status of things reflects a concrete correlation between the "symbolicness" and "thingness" and correspondingly between the symbolic and utilitarian functions. Its value is in direct proportion to "symbolicness" and in inverse proportion to "thingness". For the things comprising the material world of man it ranges widely, from minimally expressed symbolic features, when semiotic status tends to zero, to symbols-things proper with a maximum semiotic status. To give a simple example, the well-known element of the Russian oven, the shutter screen was used in two ways – for its immediate purpose and for a ritual purpose (cf. for instance, role of the shutter in the maternity, marriage and burial rituals; in the ritualised situation of searching for lost livestock and the like, where it symbolises an entrance to the afterworld with all the variety of meanings pertaining to this image). In the first case, this object functions as a thing and has minimum semiotic status; in the second case, the same object is a symbol, that is, has the highest semiotic status.

Man is constantly involved with the determining of the semiotic status of surrounding things. This is particularly evident in common views on how significant and prestigious one thing or another is, that is, how capable it is of symbolising something more important than the thing itself. As any classifying activity of a universal character, the process of determining a semiotic status is automatic and occurs, as a rule, at a subconscious level. As an instance of the perception of the semiotic non-equivalence of things, we can consider the still employed scheme of distributing objectivised elements of culture between the spheres of so called "material" and "spiritual' culture. The fact that some things are included in the sphere of "material culture" while others (no less material) are in the sphere of "spiritual culture" testifies primarily that a different semiotic status is attributed to each of them. Obviously, the things related to the sphere of "material culture" are regarded as having a low semiotic status, when the objects included in "spiritual culture" are endowed with a high semiotic status. From this point of view, "material culture" can be understood as a zone of reduced semioticity, and "spiritual culture" as that of elevated semioticity. But it should be noted that in this case an average, "normative" semiotic status is determined, built up with estimates of our experience in operating such things. It is demonstrative that each time the "material – spiritual culture" dichotomy is used, a number of objects are found that fall in neither of the spheres. An essentially similar situation can also be observed when more differentiated morphologies of culture are employed

Based on the concepts of an "average" semiotic status, the entire world of things might be placed on a scale of semioticity through conventionally marking three zones on it and classifying all objects into three unequal groups.

The upper part of the scale would be occupied by things with a constantly high semiotic status. Those may comprise, for example, masks, amulets, personal decorations, etc. In fact, these are not "things" but symbols, for their "thingness", and utility tend to zero (in any case, from the modern point of view), while "symbolicness" is most profound. Such things are usually indisputably related to "spiritual" culture.

In the lower part of the semioticity scale there would be objects with a constantly low semiotic status, i.e. things devoid of "symbolicness". This group of things can be mentioned only as applied to contemporary culture, since, based on the above specific features, the functioning of such things at earlier stages of culture is unlikely, although it is this group of things that should have comprised a sphere of material culture.

Between these two extremes of semioticity the whole scale would be occupied by the main group of things which can be used both as things and symbols (cf. for instance, symbolic functions of clothing, dwelling, utensils, food, etc.). Strictly speaking, it is only with regard to this group of things that there is any point in applying the concepts of semiotic status and scale of semioticity. Only they are things of full value. The objects conventionally referred to in the upper and lower groups are not things (i.e. do not possess the necessary integrity of symbolicness and thingness), or we have insufficient evidence to speak of their actual functioning. Therefore, it would be more correct to speak not of the three groups of things with "normatively" high, average or low semiotic status, but of which status a certain thing has in a certain context; for the same thing in another context may have a completely different degree of semioticity. This constant changing of a thing's" status, and the very possibility of its use for maintaining both biological and social being, are seen as the fundamental feature of the functioning of things in the early stages of human history.

The assessment of the semiotic status of things depends considerably on the position of a scholar who may be far removed from the real picture of the functioning of things in time, space and cultural context. At the same time, the semiotic status of one and the same thing can change significantly in time, differ for different ethnic formations and vary depending on the situation.

When considering diachronic aspects of the functioning of things an account must be taken of the following circumstance. Since the time of Taylor, Frazer and Durkheim, a contemporary scholar of the archaic world's perception begins by strictly opposing the practical and the symbolic in various ways: rational – irrational, functional – aesthetic, utilitarian – extra-utilitarian, etc. In fact, all our attempts to classify phenomena as rational and irrational are governed by a primitive scheme, whereby there are two opposite types of activity, with regard to both purposes and results. One of those produces practical effects, i.e. is aimed at satisfying the material needs of man.

The other type of activity is oriented toward extra-utilitarian (irrational) values of a symbolic nature. This activity is usually considered not only as secondary, additional to the first one, but also as non-obligatory or facultative. Such a viewpoint has become established so firmly that neither the correctness of spreading this opposition over archaic forms of culture nor even the "genuineness" of mere pragmatics are doubted. But has this division made sense at all times? Is what we now call the symbolic, extra-utilitarian and even irrational really so non-obligatory?

This paradox is known to many historians of culture. Its essence is that the most economically primitive tribes had a very complicated social organisation and an extremely developed system of rites, beliefs and myths. The strenuous efforts of those tribes were aimed, strange as it may seem, at increasing material stability and not at the extra-utilitarian sphere; they attempted to follow closely all the rites and prescriptions which were seen as a token of the collective's well-being and the essence of its existence. Why is it so? Any society fights to survive. To explain this, as is accepted among scholars of religion, by a distorted perception of the world or by a fatal delusion, would make sense only if the picture given pertained to an individual society. But since such an attitude to material production was inherent in almost any primitive society, it is hardly appropriate to speak of an accidental delusion. In this connection it is possible also to refer to a long-noted peculiarity of human culture. In the course of its history humankind detached the best people for the non-practical, extra-utilitarian activity (Lotman 1970: 3–4). And if it is so, "it is hard to assume that it lacked an organic necessity, that humankind would systematically give up the vitally necessary for the facultative. It may be assumed that while for the biological existence of an individual man it would suffice to satisfy certain natural needs, the life of a collective, as such, is impossible without a culture. For any collective, culture is not a facultative addition to a minimum of life conditions but rather an indispensable situation without which its being is impossible" (Lotman 1970: 4).

In fact, the existence of the second, social, or symbolic pragmatics is the point. When in the "practical – symbolic" scheme we are based on the presence of one sort of needs – "utilitarian", then, in the connection with the above ideas, needs equally important for a man's social life can be of two types – utilitarian and symbolic. The main difference between them is that the former necessitate an immediate satisfaction and cannot be amassed while the latter reveal a capacity for accumulation.

"They represent an objective foundation for an organism to retrieve extra-genetic information. As a result, two types of attitude of the organism toward introduced alien structures emerge: the first ones transform themselves immediately or relatively quickly into the structure of the organism itself; others are stored with their own structure preserved or somewhat curtailed. Whether we deal with a material accumulation of objects or with a memory in its short or long-term, personal or collective forms, in fact, we face one and the same process which can be defined as a process of increase of information" (Lotman 1970: 5).

So, it can be stated quite safely that there are two sorts of pragmatics: utilitarian and symbolic. It is important to stress once again that the two pragmatics are vitally important when we speak of the social aspect of human activity, and in this sense symbolic pragmatics are as "practical" as "utilitarian".

The recognition that symbolic pragmatics are vitally important is the first step toward a revision of established schemes of interpreting an archaic culture. Strictly speaking, this statement is of a universal nature, since it can be applied to any social formation, both archaic and modern. Differences, and rather profound ones, lie in the sphere of predominant orientation toward this or that type of pragmatics, in methods of organising the utilitarian and symbolic activities, and in the nature of their correlation.

The overturning in world perception (transition from cosmology to history) whose characteristics are becoming clearer now, is likely to have been associated quite closely with the re-orientation of man and the collective towards the other type of pragmatics. The "straightening" of time and the perception of its irreversibility was accompanied by a global restructuring of cosmological principles. The foreground of life worthy of being described, is taken by man with his needs, concerns and everyday deeds. While in the cosmological age the purpose and sense of life were seen in a ritual and routine existence that filled in intervals between rituals, the historical world perception, along with the seeds of scientific vision, was oriented primarily not toward symbolic but practical values. Of course, this is not to say that one type of pragmatics was replaced by the other. They have co-existed for ever. We can speak only about prevailing tendencies and appraisals. Whereas for primitive man utilitarian pragmatics were just a required condition for performing paramount, sacred objectives, modern man is inclined to go too far in the direction by regarding symbolic activity simply as an appendix to the main economic one.

The extreme rationalism of a modern, primarily scientific perception of the world, has trained us to a firm belief not only that symbolic activity is secondary, but also that the clear division between the utilitarian and symbolic aspects was always there. However, this is not true even with regard to contemporary culture. As was stated above, many things of utilitarian purpose have also additional (aesthetic, prestigious) significance. It is incorrect to speak about a dichotomy of the utilitarian and symbolic with regard to phenomena of archaic culture, especially when we use oppositions such as "rational – irrational".

Where are the criteria for distinguishing between the rational and irrational? By granting such a division, we start from establishments of our own culture. But it is known that the internal and external viewpoints on rationality may differ. What is seen as rational from the point of view of one culture may be regarded as irrational from that of another. Those scholars are definitely correct who think that every society considers the main manifestations of its social life as rational(Chernykh 1982:10). In other words, such a division is always subjective. But the matter is, whether it is at all possible to operate such oppositions in regard to an archaic culture? Even if yes, this inevitably leads to a negative answer. The same can be said with regard to other antinomies with which we are used to describing not only our own world but also the world of primitive man (Frankfort et al. 1967:13). Turning back to pragmatic orientations at early stages of culture, it should be noted that the correlation of "thingness" and "symbolicness" does not suggest the posing of the question of "what is initial and what secondary" due to the fact that these two properties are complimentary (as left-right, top-bottom, etc.). This circumstance requires a prudent treatment of the hypotheses in accordance with which the origins of things are connected exclusively with practical or exclusively with symbolic needs of man. The thing becomes a fact of culture only when it meets both practical and symbolic requirements. In this connection, for instance, an idea of A. Leroi-Gourhan (1965: 139) seems to be absolutely correct, that only when a dwelling is ascribed a symbolic meaning can one speak of it as a specifically human form of exploring the environment (as opposed to the "perimeter of safety" which exists among animals).

The segregation of different types of human activities from the syncretic system, and their specialisation, were accompanied by a decrease in the role of sacred beliefs and correspondingly by an increase in the relative significance of the productive and instrumental aspects of these activities followed by significant changes in the structure of semiotic systems used by a society. The boundary between semiotic and non-semiotic phenomena becomes clearer. The semioticity of things in contemporary culture has decreased sharply, and for many of these things it is no longer an obligatory property.

Let us attempt to consider more closely an informative aspect of the functions of things. In his pioneer study on functions of folk costume, P.G. Bogatyrev showed authoritatively that any thing in "folk" everyday life has a whole spectrum of functions: practical, social, aesthetic, magical, regional identity and several others (Bogatyrev 1971: 297). Depending on the situation, these functions fall into one order or another: some of them increase, while others remain in the background. For example, in daily life practical function dominates, followed by (for folk clothing) the social, aesthetic, and regional identity functions. Another hierarchy of the functions is typical of a festive occasion: the festive, aesthetic, ceremonial, national and regional identity, social and, finally, practical, certain elements of a festive garment lacking any practical significance. In other words, depending on the situation the whole structure of functions changes to cause a qualitative shift in the functioning and perception of things: having remained the same, it nevertheless becomes different. This effect of "differentness" of things was labelled by P.G. Bogatyrev as a "structure of functions", which "cannot be deduced from all other functions that make up the structure in general" (Bogatyrev 1971: 357). In his defining of this function and in pointing out its proximity to the functions of national in regional identity (our people, our social group, our dress), P.G. Bogatyrev was close to an acute but still unexplored problem of ethnic symbols, ethnicity and ethnographicity.

It is fundamental for the structure of functions to distinguish between the energetic (practical function according to P.G. Bogatyrev) and the communicative aspects. It is a result of the segregation of the communicative aspect of things that gives the entire collection of functions, apart from the practical which is the only one to represent an integral and further undivided energetic aspect.

The energetic and communicative aspects of things correspond with the notions of "thingness" and "symbolicness" which we have used in describing semiotic status. With regard to the structure of functions proposed by P.G. Bogatyrev, the semiotic status of a thing is directly dependent on the place it occupies according to the practical function. To describe, in turn, the informative characteristics of things it seems useful to conditionally distinguish between two forms of their functioning – everyday and ritual. In the first case, a thing functions as a text, and in the latter as a symbol. What does this mean?

The Thing as a Text

Properly speaking, it is this aspect that was described by P.G. Bogatyrev in terms of function. When we speak of a thing as a text, we mean all the information which is communicated by things; more specifically, that which can be "retrieved" from the things themselves in a usual situation, for instance, by an archaeologist or a museum curator. What sort of information could we obtain?

Firstly, information on what class of things (utensils, decorations, etc.) this thing can be related to. Thus, the functional purpose of the thing can be determined approximately.

Secondly, information on what makes it different from the rest of things in the class, i.e. its individual features and purpose. The latter is of special significance in those cases in which the thing with known practical purpose happens to be found in a context which makes us suppose that the thing might have been used for other purposes (for instance, tools in burials).

Thirdly, if the given thing is comparable to many other things of the class by its formal traits, the technique and especially decoration used, we can make an assumption of its belonging to an ethnic group, archaeological culture or style. When a thing is purposely made and used as a sign of one's culture (ethnicity, ethnic group, etc.), its functional aspect becomes narrower and its semiotic status becomes higher.

Fourthly, one can speak not only of a historical dating of things but, no less important, of its relation to historically different models of culture, when possible. The life of things and their semiotic destiny have never been the subject of investigation. If we try to imagine a synchronous section of the object level of culture, we shall have a colourful picture of things. Some are already extinct and are not used for their immediate purpose. Still others may be used as a "memory" for prestigious, ritual and other purposes. A third group may function actively, while the rest are only in the beginning of their unpredictable life. In general, old things have a paradoxical destiny – they are either destroyed or gain the highest semiotic status to be used exclusively for symbolic purposes. New things have not occupied a place (and possibly will never do so, which is also very significant) in the culture. The historical value of all these things, as well as the volume of their historical and cultural memory, differ considerably, and the more precise our knowledge of this aspect of the life of things, the more informative the things are, for they represent the most reliable channel which connects us with the past.

Fifthly, a thing can tell not only of its maker (and, correspondingly, of the level of technological development and methods) but also of its owner, his/her preferences, tendencies and orientations. In these terms, the most demonstrative element is clothing. By it we can judge the gender, age and social status of the owner. But these features are demonstrated by any dress. Its informational capacity increases sharply only when clothing points to the listed universal (and therefore uninformative) indices of any society and also to secondary features of social organisation (for instance, a costume of a herder, a smith and other sub-cultural associations; it is these features that are typical of the Moravian costume described by P.G. Bogatyrev). It should be kept in mind that many things, especially at later stages of cultural development, may be used as signs of prestige and not for their immediate purposes. In such cases the usefulness of a thing and its practical purpose shift to the background or are not taken into account at all.

Finally, there is a specific class of things whose value is intrinsic, in their existence. They include paintings, works of folk art, architecture, jewellery, etc. Contrary to other things, their value but grows over time. Becoming older, they grow in significance. Things valuable in themselves represent a rare type of signs – they denote themselves and not something external. Even if they were supposed to function as symbols, they are not so in reality, for they "refer" to themselves. Their significance is "much broader than the thing itself and it bears an infinite character; simultaneously, this significance is oriented toward the very thing and only toward it" (Segal 1986: 41).

The Thing as a Symbol

In considering a thing as a symbol, we "read" the upper surface layer of information. The innermost significance of things reveals itself in the ritual and ritualised situation. This significance does not come from the things themselves. It can be detected only by turning to the sources external to things.

If a thing functions or may function in everyday life as a text, then in a ritual it also may be used as a *symbol*. It should also be kept in mind that in a traditional society everyday life is ritualised to a considerable extent and has a system of connotations in common with a ritual. That is why the everyday use of things implies their being used for utilitarian purposes.

All the information which may be obtained from the everyday state of things, takes the background in the ritual and ritualised situations. In a ritual, the semiotic status of things increases profoundly. This effect takes place due to the fact that in a ritual all customary characteristics of things change, and so do their *pragmatics, semantics* and *syntactics.*

What is the purpose of things-symbols in a ritual? Before answering this question, we should say a few words about the general tendency of ritual. As noted above, the type of culture for which a ritual is the main tool of regulating behaviour of man and a collective, can be characterised by its integrity and unity. This means that any phenomenon within any one sphere causes changes in other spheres. For such a culture the division of the world into one's own, explored sphere and the alien, or unexplored, is fundamental, the latter being a concentration of powers beyond the control of common means (gods, ancestors, etc.). Any violation of the order is followed by a change in relationship between these two worlds, as well as the existing *status quo*. The lost harmony can be re-established with the help of a corresponding ritual. From this standpoint, the ritual is a particular mechanism of balancing. In order to achieve the desired equilibrium, a contact is established in the ritual between one's own sphere and the alien, since the violation is more often regarded as a consequence of the destructive powers of the "alien" sphere. In other words, the ritual embraces a new "agreement" and thus a world order is re-established which corresponds to the initial sacred pattern.

Ritual is a unique and universal means of both the re-establishing of harmony and the test (control) of the correspondence of the variety of links to how it was "for the first time". Naturally, the solution of such a complicated task is impossible without the mobilisation of all means of expressiveness in the possession of the collective. According to V.N. Toporov, such a "parade of sign systems" in the ritual is necessary to give it maximum effectiveness in re-establishing lost equilibrium and control over the world.

To achieve this goal, the ritual aims at necessarily re-establishing the world in its unity and integrity. It is this that all symbolic means used in the ritual are levelled at. Every "language" used in the ritual (words, gestures, actions, objects, landscape parts, etc.) seems to have had its own specialisation, i.e. transmitted certain information about the world. The language of things is likely to have been used primarily for expressing the ideas, concepts and values which could not be expressed as adequately in other languages, including that of words. Such "inexpressible" ideas include the concepts of "alien" and the concepts of such paramount life values as destiny, well-being, fertility, posterity, etc. All these concepts gained, through object symbols, a concrete and tangible form. It was possible to literally touch them by hand, and, in the event when they objectivated powers of the alien world, to establish necessary relations with and a control over them.

This function of things was called by V. Turner (1975: 15) a *revelation*. In comparing the revelation with divination, another method to "make visible" what is covert, he writes that *revelation* is the disclosure, under the conditions of a ritual and through symbolic actions and means, of all that cannot be expressed and classified with words. Thus, divination represents a method of analysis and a taxonomical system, while revelation is an envelopment of experience in general.

Such observations are in conflict with the wide-spread point of view on the synonymous character and inter-dependence of ritual symbols and the corresponding "languages" (Tolstoy 1982: 57–71). It is likely that there is every reason to suggest a particular specialisation of semiotic systems used in the ritual for transmitting certain information. For example, in some regional traditions the denial of matchmaking employs exclusively an "object language": the match-makers are handed a watermelon (or a pumpkin), sourdough is loaded on their wagon, etc. On the contrary, such a specialisation has limitations of using other languages. The same suggestion can be formulated in a different way: every "language" has its strong position in the syntagmatic structure of the ritual, where it possesses the priority right to code information. For example, the theme of farewell to girlhood in the Russian wedding is realised primarily in songs and lamentations, and the fact of chastity (or non-chastity) is transmitted predominantly through object symbols. All other "languages" into which the information is translated (or can be translated) would have a secondary role (translations of the original).

Thus, the hierarchy of "languages" in the ritual is variable. It has a profound situational character. In some strands of the ritual object symbols dominate, in others – verbal symbols, while in a third – mental images, etc. Despite the accepted axiom stating that the choice of a language (code) is not dependent on the transmitted contents, it is the contents actualised during the given fraction of the ritual that are most likely to determine (or even assign automatically) the usage of a certain manner of expression. It is too early to speak about whatever correlation between the character of information and semiotic systems may be employed in the ritual, but as to object symbols, in the context of the ritual they are most "adjusted" to denote the states (status) of characters or to express the most general ideas (lot, fertility, wealth, one's own, alien, etc.). This results in their characterising, determining function. At the same time, a verbal language is more often used when ideas of passage from one state to another are actualised, that which, as a rule, is accompanied by a change of characteristics. But similar observations need to be considerably elaborated, which implies a special investigation in this direction.

The main opposition of the ritual (one's own – alien, in various modifications) and the task of relieving the strain between these two worlds preconditioned the usage of things for the following purposes:

First, with their help both the "own" and the "alien" are symbolised. In principle, any cultural symbol (i.e. a man-made object) relates to the world of man and denotes this world. Nevertheless, in every tradition there is a set of things that are used in the ritual exclusively with this aim to embody the idea of "own" to a greater extent than the rest. As a rule, those are the objects which are placed in the centre, inside one's own world: in the house, in "the red corner", by the hearth or in another sacred (and the innermost) place. It can be the very hearth, a loaf of bread baked on it, charcoal, litter, etc.

Contrary to this, objects used in the ritual for denoting the "alien" are usually placed in the periphery of the man-explored space or on the boundary between the "own" and "alien". And, since this boundary is not absolute, elements of clothing, parts of the house (walls, windows, doors, chimney), as well as off-centre constructions (bath, fence) may be used as a border line. Another class of objects frequently used for the same purpose are objects newly made and not completely introduced into the "own" sphere, as noted above, as well as old broken and therefore partly "own" objects.

The other and most well-known function of things in ritual is to be an instrument of connecting the two worlds. The use of things as mediators is based, with all probability, on the known duality: on the one hand, any thing belongs to the world of nature (material for their production comes from there); on the other hand, it has been subjected to special operations, bringing it from the sphere of the natural to the sphere of the artificial, man-processed and therefore integrated into the culture. By the way, it is this circumstance that can explain the presence of opposing meanings of things with the function of ritual symbols, as described by V. Turner and other scholars. Maximum mediative capability is typical of the so called universal sign complexes: the cross, an object symbolising the world tree, temple, etc., which lie next to the sphere of "another" and possess a paramount modelling function.

Finally, an opposing function of things-symbols should also be noted. It consists in the fact that they "bar" or block the communication channel between the "own" and the "alien". It is this function that the so called amulets perform to demarcate a symbolic (and therefore the most effective) boundary between humans and the powers of the outer world. In the process, the link between these spheres gains a regulated character, and a possibility of control over it by man emerges.

We have merely touched on some issues of the pragmatics of things. The semantics and syntactics will be examined in another essay.

References

Antonova, E.V. 1984: *Ocherki kultury drevnikh zemledeltsev Perednei i Srednei Azii*. Moskva.

Averintsev, S.S. 1977: *Poetica rannevizantiyskoy literatury*. Moskva.

Baiburin, Albert 1981: Semioticheskiy status veschey. In: *Material'naya kultura i mifologiya. Sbornik statey Museya antropologii i etnografii*. Vol. 1.

Baiburin, Albert 1983: *Zhilische v kul'ture russkogo naroda*. Leningrad.

Bogatyrev, P.G. 1971: *Voprosy teorii narodnogo iskusstva*. Moskva.

Chernykh, E.I. Proyavleniya ratsionalnogo i irratsionalnogo v arkheologicheskoy kulture. In: *Soviet Archaeology*, 1982, No. 4.

Frankfort, H. and H.A., Wilson, John, Jacobsen, Thorkild 1967: *Before Philosophy. The Intellectual Adventure of Ancient Man*. Baltimore.

Ivanov, V.V. 1983: *Istoriya slavyanskikh i balkanskikh nazvaniy metallov*. Moskva.

Kultura drevnego Egipta. Moskva, 1976.

Leroi-Gourhan, A. 1965: *Le geste et la parole*. Paris, vol. 2.

Lévi-Strauss, Claude 1972: *Structural Anthropology*. Harmondsworth.

Lévi-Strauss, Claude 1973: *The Savage mind*. Chicago.

Lotman, Yuriy M. 1970: *Statii po tipologii kultury*. Tartu, issue 1.

Segal, D.M. 1986: *Mir veschei i semiotica*. No. 4.

Tolstoy, Nikita I. 1982: Iz "grammatiki" slavyanskikh obryadov. In: *Statii po znakovym sistemam*. Tartu, issue 15.

Toporov, V.N. 1982: Pervobytnyie predstavleniya o mire: obschiy vzglyad. In: *Ocherki po istorii estestvenno-nauchnykh znaniy v antichnosti*. Moskva.

Toporov, V.N. 1983: Prostranstvo i tekst. In: *Tekst: Semantika i Struktura*. Moskva.

Turner, V.W. 1975: *Revelation and Divination in Ndembu Ritual*. Ithaca and London.

Vinogradov, G.S. 1918: Materialy dlya narodnogo kalendarya russkogo starozhilogo naseleniya Sibiri. In: *Zapiski Tulukovskogo obschestva po Izucheniyu Sibiri i uluchsheniyu domashnei zhizni*. Irkutsk, issue 1.

The Commercialization of Childhood

Helene Brembeck and Barbro Johansson

Brembeck, Helene and Johansson, Barbro 1997: The Commercialization of Childhood. – Ethnologia Europaea 27: 15–28.

Commercialism has left its mark on all aspects of children's everyday lives today. It constitutes a shared world of experience, permeating relations between children and within the family. The article discusses the possibilities of an in-depth analysis from an ethnological perspective. One possibility is to study commercialization from the children's perspective as practice, social activity, or lifestyle. This is exemplified primarily with children's computer games. Another possibility is to study in a historical perspective how consumerism has been gradually introduced, established, institutionalized, and finally made into a seemingly self-evident part of the children's world. The authors discuss how the process could be studied through archival sources such as advertisements and price-lists. The article concludes with a discussion of the new images of family relations and children's competences that emerge from the commercial media. In advertisements for computers, children are presented as competent and superior. In television series, parents are often portrayed as pathetic, as clumsy fathers and nagging mothers, while the children are enterprising and crafty. What does that say about actual changes in family relations and problems in today's families?

Helene Brembeck, Ph.D., and Barbro Johansson, doctoral student, Department of Ethnology, Gothenburg University, S–412 98 Göteborg, Sweden. E-mail:Helene.Brembeck@ethnology.gu.se

Commercialism has created a world of signs and symbols that in many respects is the first world with which children come into contact today, a world that becomes virtually as real as the actual world out there. Helene found an example one day on her way home, when she saw a notice stuck to a lamp-post, and further on another one, both with the same message: "Has anyone seen my cat Ludde? He looks just like the cat in the Pussi ad. Please call ..." followed by the name and telephone number of the eleven-year-old owner. Just a few decades ago, lost animals would have been described in a completely different way, in terms of colour, markings, and distinctive features, with comparisons taken from the world of nature. For today's children, designations such as lime-blossom green or straw-coloured scarcely have any relevance, but a comparison to "the cat in the Pussi ad" does. The cat that advertises Pussi cat food is not just any cat. It is a black cat with a white nose, the white mark running up and tapering in the shape of the Eiffel Tower. The Pussi cat is a celebrity for many children today. It lives its own life in television commercials and has its own personality, in a way that gives the tins on the supermarket shelf a special charge. Learning and interpreting the symbolic world of advertising is as essential for a child as understanding the underlying process by which the meat ends up in the tin.

In consumption studies this shared world of experience is often primarily described as a symbolic world associated with an accelerated post-modernization of culture. This symbolism provides models, language, signs to play with, and dreams, wishes, fantasies to be charmed by and urged to realize. The example above shows that there is a great deal of truth in this description. Yet commercialization cannot be understood solely as an illusory world floating above the real world, available to those who seek inspiration for an escape from reality or an identity construction. It is much more pervasive than that.

To begin with, the symbols of commercialism are a shared world of experience for children today to play with and associate with. When our children meet their holiday friends once again and have to find something to talk about on the long summer evenings, with no television or video, there are two natural topics of conversation: their favourite comics in the Disney magazine, and the cartoons and advertisements on television: best, worst, most exciting, corniest, neatest graphics, best music, and so on. Everyone can join in, associating, talking and laughing, even if there are a few years' difference in age or if the gang consists of both girls and boys.

Commercialism also pervades relations between children. In the children's world there are often different styles, and children have clear perceptions of what is neatest or corniest, best or worst, cutest or ugliest. The symbolic value of things gives the potential to express something about who one is or wants to be, which world one wants to express solidarity with or from which one wishes to dissociate oneself. At the age of just eight, children are fully fledged consumers, as Stephen Kline says in *Out of the Garden: Toys, TV and Children's Culture in the Age of Marketing* (1993). They know all about the range of goods on offer in the convenience store, they know how to convert their pocket-money into hard currency in the children's world in the form of ice hockey cards, sweets, and scented erasers.

Commercialism also makes its mark on relations between parents and children. Parents buy things for their children as a token of their love and affinity, to reward and to delight, perhaps to salve a guilty conscience about not being at home enough or not having enough time for the children. The children soon learn negotiation techniques. Appealing to the symbolic value of objects as pleasure, consolation, protection against guilty consciences, pointing out that "everyone else has ...", and hence playing on the parents' fears that their children will be left outside, ostracized, or bullied. Or collecting activity points by making beds, sweeping floors, taking out the rubbish, points which can then be converted into money with which to buy things and hence fulfil oneself.

Commercialism thus pervades and affects all parts of children's lives today. It forms a shared frame of reference and affects the perception of the surrounding world. It permeates games and relations in children's culture. It sets its stamp on relations to the adult world. It penetrates identity formation, serving as a reference point for the child's perception of who he is. It creates dreams and frustrations about what is best, biggest, and most beautiful. And it always indicates the same solutions when the images of how one should act, look, or dress become too contradictory or deviate too much from the everyday reality in which children live – consume more, something different, something new! Commercialism is not something we can ignore. It is an integral part of our everyday lives today, whether we like it or not. That is why it has been said that the ideology of post-modernity is *consumerism*, which means that consumption is more than an activity; it is a way of life and thus indissolubly connected to identity. The identity of post-modern man is linked to consumption, not to production as it used to be. The time is long gone since we consumed solely for our material needs. According to Baudrillard (Bocock 1993), it is primarily emotional needs that today's consumer tries to satisfy.

How did it end up this way? How are we to perceive "this brave new world" in which we live, with all its commercialism? And how can we as ethnologists contribute to an understanding of this world, what it does to us and our children, and what we do to it? These were the questions we considered in our work with the anthology *Postmodern barndom* ("Post-modern Childhood", Brembeck and Johansson 1996), for which the students were sent out to document different "post-modern tendencies" in today's childhood. It was shown time and again that commercialism was at the centre.

Consumption as Lifestyle

One way to take the pulse of today's childhood is to get under the surface, to investigate opinions and attitudes from the perspective of the users, the children and the parents, and to see commercialism not just as a structure or dimension but also as a practice. Is it possible to trace consumerism in present-day children's consumption? Yes, for we can see how the advertisers succeed in their purpose: to get the children to want to have a multitude of products which they do not need in material terms. We who were small in the 1960s perhaps had a Barbie and a Ken that we bought clothes for. The girls of the 1990s, in contrast, buy and ask for new dolls all the time. Even if they already have twelve Barbie dolls, they still want that special "Party Barbie", or "Pocahontas" or "Riding Barbie" that they have seen in the alluring advertisements. With her new clothes, her accessories, and special attributes such as the length and colour of her hair or the colour of her skin, each doll has an individual personality. The doll is more than the wearer of a set of clothes; it offers a role, an identity. Barbie is the postmodern dream of changing identity as easily as one changes clothes.

Another way in which consumption satisfies emotional needs is by becoming a social activity, for example, a shared family activity. Instead of a walk in the forest, the family can spend a Saturday afternoon at the shopping mall. When children play together, their play requires them to have the same toys or to watch the same television programmes. A special case is the ice hockey cards that children collect, swap, buy, and sell. It is nothing new for children to collect things, nor that there are obvious economic incentives; collections of stamps and coins can acquire a high value. What is new about ice hockey cards is that the trade in the pictures has become as important as the actual collecting, thus showing a clear similarity to adult speculation in stocks and shares – an example of boundaries between generations being transcended.

Consumerism thus means that the concept of consumption is broadened. Until now we have mentioned the expanded symbolic meaning of the consumed products. The goods stand for much more than their practical use, they have an important symbolic function. This is a necessary condition if consumption is to be a lifestyle. In addition, there has been an expansion of the things encompassed by consumption. What was formerly connected to the individual's personality and perhaps did not change through a whole lifetime – such as taste, style, interests, political and religious affiliation – is now an object for consumption. Everything becomes a commodity and hence can be exchanged, even one's own identity.

Using the Media

When one speaks of the commercialization of childhood, about the power of advertising over children and the heavy impact of the media, it is easy to take the view that children are victims. This has long been the common attitude in media studies. Scholars have studied what has gone *into* the children in the form of violence, action, and stereotyped pictures, and then what has come *out* in the form of aggressive behaviour, anxiety, and prejudice. In recent years, however, many scholars have rejected this view of children as passive receivers and instead studied the effect of advertising and the media as an active process from the children's side as well. There is of course no reason to try to deny that children are influenced by what they see, hear, and experience – the whole school system is based on this – but the perspective changes if the child is placed as an active subject in the centre of the process. In particular, this makes it much easier to understand why children are influenced to such different extents. Of four children who see a violent scene on television, one may be inspired to go out and fight, while another may be upset and reject violence, a third may find inspiration for a game, while the fourth may be wholly unaffected. It all depends on the circumstances of the child.

These circumstances, however, should not be reduced to an individual psychological level. The repertoire and the options are not infinite in the culture of which the child is part, and the things that children, each in their own way, practise and learn to manage as well as possible in the society in which they live.

What is it that the children learn, what do they practise, what is it that they need to bring out in life? Whereas man's task in the early days of industrial society was to do one's work in the factory as quickly and efficiently as possible, with no unnecessary talk, in our later industrial society it is instead a matter of solving problems, discussion, communicating, arriving at the solutions together. Since much of what is produced is information, it is obvious that the

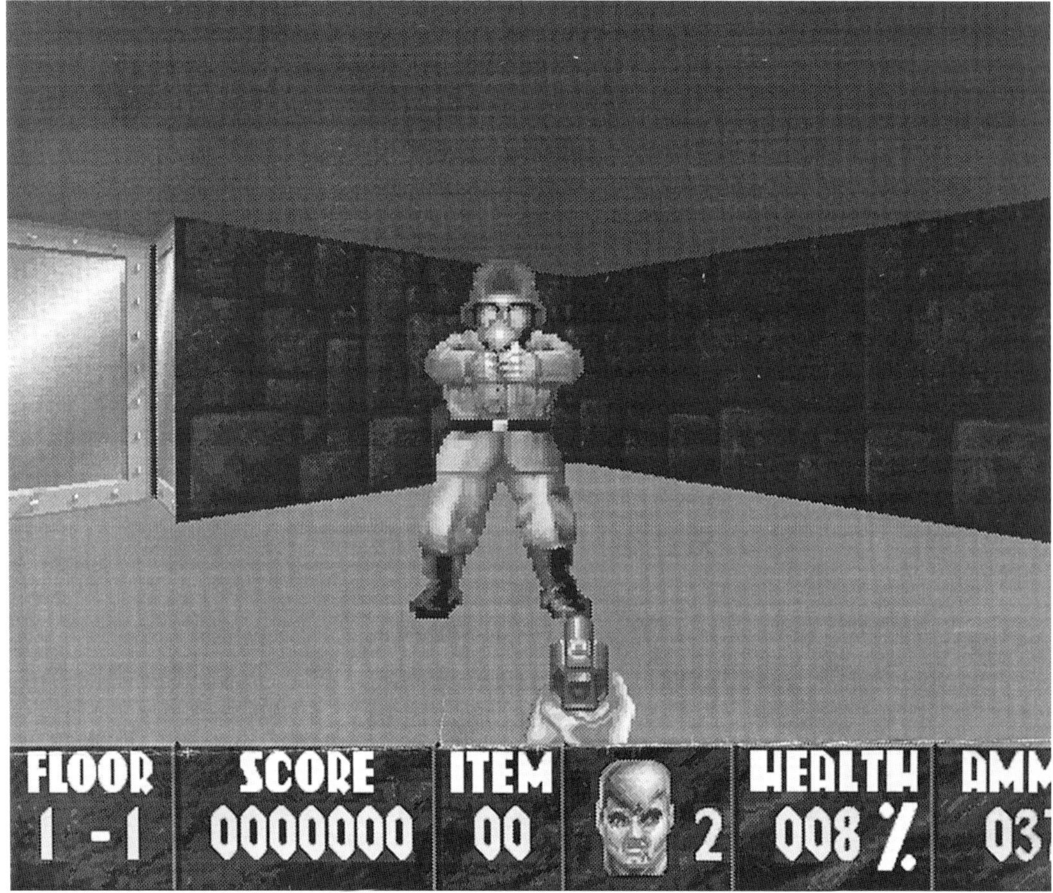

Fig. 1. There is no simple association between media violence and aggressive behaviour in children. Most children make a sharp distinction between playing violent games and using real violence. This picture is from the computer game *Wolfenstein*, in which the player fights Nazis in a German bunker. The player's own injuries are shown in a box.

skill that is valued most highly today is communicative competence (Frönes 1987).

Children practise this competence in their games, which is why games today look very different from games in the past (Rönnberg 1987). Children today live in small nuclear families and rarely have any insight into their parents' jobs. The media are therefore an important source for understanding the world. It may seem as if there is a contradiction in the claim that children actively construct themselves and acquire communicative competence in interaction with other people, while at the same time they spend so many hours seemingly passive in front of the television set or the computer. Yet Rönnberg (1987) argues that, even if children are physically passive in front of the television, they are creative and active on the mental level. According to Rönnberg, television gives rise to two different kinds of play. There is play on the mental level, a game of thought or a looking game. In addition, the media function as a collectively shared play model, serving as a basis for "media games" when the television is switched off.

The media can thus be said to favour communicative competence by functioning as a model and as a knowledge bank. As a model, the media inform us about how communication takes place. The children get ideas and suggestions as to what to do and how to behave in encounters with others. As a knowledge bank, the media supply children with shared frames of reference which can serve as a basis for communication between them. They can play Björne (a man dressed as a bear in a favourite Swedish children's television programme) or Power Rangers, and they can invent their own commercials based on television advertising.

A Good Childhood

Behind every advertisement that children and their parents meet, there are a number of assumptions about the world which the receivers are expected to share. Let us take a product that is now spreading like wildfire in schools and families, with the support of intensive marketing: the computer. There is a generally accepted view that the computer is a thing of the future. "What your children need to know for the future, they can now learn in their spare time" is the slogan used by Futurekids in their advertisement, playing on the Swedish words *framtid* "future" and *fritid* "leisure time". It is not just in advertisements but also in articles about children and computers that the connection between computers and future is made to appear self-evident. A school in which the children use computers is called "the school of the future" and the children are called "the children of the future", although all this obviously takes place in the present. And the latest computer technology is said to be "only the beginning"; after just a few years, computer models are antiquated. In addition, we are constantly reminded that we must hurry. "Full speed ahead. Those who don't keep up only have themselves to blame" (Hadenius 1995). It is essential not to miss the train and be left on the platform among the losers in the computer society.

Yet there is also a discourse to the opposite effect, which argues that "children must be allowed to be children". It is felt to be fundamentally unnatural that children sit in front of a computer screen instead of being outside climbing trees, building little houses, and playing tag. Instead of emphasizing the importance of children having sharp elbows and getting to the future as fast as possible, this view urges that they should have opportunities for play, fantasy, and peace and quiet, in contrast to the dazzling, high-speed multimedia effects of the computer world.

It is easy to see this complex of ideas as a reaction to the "future discourse", and it is obvious that the two discourses stand out more clearly as a result of the polarization between them. In order to better understand what happens, however, it is important to see that these opposed ideas have not arisen in our days with the introduction of computers for children. We can trace the historical roots back in time, to see how new techniques have always created great expectations – in the 1960s (which was symptomatically called the space age), for example, people dreamed of a small space rocket for every family – and have always encountered reactions in the form of fears, critique, and usually anxiety about how this will affect the children. The reaction has often taken the form of moral panic, which has been provoked by videos, television, comics, and even children's books when they started to appear. Back in the eighteenth century Rousseau warned of the danger of letting children learn to read, since it would mean the end of the innocent and natural childhood. There is thus a deep-rooted dichotomy between "the natural" and "the artificial", and even between nature and culture, a dichotomy which can also be taken as a starting point for defining a "good childhood".

Reading History from Advertisements

A fascinating point of departure for a continued study of the commercialization of childhood would therefore be to take a step backwards and study the present in the light of history. A tested ethnological method for understanding something complex and contradictory of which we ourselves as modern people are part is to study the phenomenon as a stage in a process in which the "roots" and part of the explanation lie one or perhaps more generations in the past. One way is to apply the "formation perspective" advocated by Orvar Löfgren (1990). This means that the focus is on how new phenomena are formed, established, institutionalized, routinized, and eventually taken for granted, trivialized, or mystified.

Here too, we have a multitude of possible

methods and materials, many of which have been successfully tested in the Lund project "Welfare Dreams and Everyday Life: Consumption in Post-war Sweden", under Löfgren's leadership (e.g. Löfgren 1992, 1993, 1996). In our continued work we shall confine ourselves exclusively to archival material such as advertisements, price-lists, books of advice, and so on in the field of toys, children's fashions, and children's use of the media. Part of the reason for this is that we start our study in 1900. The decades around the turn of the century have been described as a period of upheaval in the field of children's culture (e.g. Kline 1993). Industrialization and industrial technology had attained a level that enabled mass production. The increased range of goods reached families in all social classes – not just the rich – and they could all increasingly afford it.

It may be wondered what can be derived from advertisements apart from the fact that they function like the "tradesmen's entrances" that Löfgren (1990) recommends, like "peepholes" into a culture or "texts" from which we can read a society. Do they give us any information that we could not get elsewhere? Can we really arrive at a deeper understanding of the complex reality in which children live today by studying, for example, toy advertisements from the 1930s, pram advertisements from the 1910s, or sweet advertisements from the 1950s? As Löfgren (1996) has pointed out, reading culture as a text has proved to be "a narrow and one-dimensional metaphor for the multifaceted character of everyday culture". With the articles in *Postmodern barndom* in mind, we can only agree with this. At the same time, we believe that an advertisement for, say, toys or children's clothes must be understood as something more powerful than just a "text".

Teddy Bears for Good Children

Let us look at an advertisement for a teddy bear from 1903 by the Steiff Toy Manufacturing Company. It shows a small girl in a white dress hugging a giant teddy bear, gently leaning her cheek against its shaggy head. How should we understand an advertisement like this? First of all, it is an expression of the societal and ideological changes occurring at the turn of the century.[1]

Fig. 2. "What parent can resist granting his child the joy that a teddy bear brings?" Steiff advertisement from 1903.

Industrialization and urbanization had drastically affected the social position of children. Most children in towns – possibly with the exception of the very poorest strata of the working class – were no longer involved in working life. They were on the contrary released from work, and it was the responsibility of society, or at least the adult world, to lead them on to the right track. It could be said that childhood as a cultural category was created now, not just for the children of the bourgeoisie but also for broad groups of children, at least in the cities. Parallel to this, the concept of "child" was recharged in bourgeois circles during the nineteenth century. Whereas children had previously been regarded as blank slates to be filled with knowledge, as bearers of original sin, or as small adults who just needed to grow in strength and knowledge to be able to enter adult roles, in the nineteenth century there arose a rival, romanticized view of children – or at least bourgeois children – as pure and unspoiled, good through and through, the bearers of a superior morality, God's angels on earth.

At the same time, there arose the idea of the excellence of toys. Bourgeois children were to be educated, stimulated, and trained from their very first years to assimilate all the bourgeois virtues and attain the same economic and social position as their parents. Toys were perceived as excellent aids to this end. This applied in particular to the abundance of educational toys that began to fill the bourgeois nurseries towards the end of the nineteenth century, such as games, mechanical kits, steam engines, and peep-shows (Bjurman 1981:104). Even very young infants, who had been of very little interest to secular and ecclesiastical authorities and had scarcely been perceived even by their parents as being educable, were now to be exposed to education and intensive stimulation.

With the breakthrough of Freudian psychology around 1900, infancy came to be regarded as the most significant phase of childhood, when a child had to be subjected to intensive education. The child was at the mercy of drives which had to be channelled in the right direction. Incorrect action on the part of the parents could have devastating consequences for the child later in life. Although psychology stressed the importance of emotional intimacy and warmth, too much "corporeality" and fondling between parent and child was viewed negatively. The baby had to cope on its own even in the cradle, and be able to occupy itself for long periods alone in the nursery. The practice of having the nanny sleep with the children was abandoned, and the nursery became a private, secluded children's land, supervised from a distance by the nanny (Kildegaard Hansen 1987).

On top of this came the mass launching of factory-made toys. In this way one can find a multitude of explanations for the specific design of the Steiff teddy bear advertisement. Yet this cannot solely be understood as a reflection of the contemporary social and ideological climate; it is also in large measure a human construction. The increased use of technology in industry, new conditions for the children of the bourgeoisie, a new view of children – all this might have had little effect if there had been no marketers. Without them, the production of teddy bears would scarcely have increased with the incredible speed that it did: from the first teddy bear at the toy fair in Leipzig in 1903 until a production volume of 974,000 bears just three years later.

The Loving Comrade

In the same way as advertisers today, the Steiff family's advertising designers enlisted all the contemporary psychological theories to try to convince parents of the necessity of toys. A central aspect of all toy marketing is to give the object meanings which were not originally there. The marketers thus tried to give the teddy bear a symbolic charge, listening attentively to "the needs of the market" so that they could strike the right chord.

The picture painted by Steiff and other large toy manufacturers was of the teddy bear as a loving comrade and companion, not just in childhood but throughout life. A soft, cuddly friend, always by your side, with whom you can share your sorrows and joys, a good listener, always willing to comfort you in childhood when you have been scolded by mother, in your teens when your boyfriend has let you down, or in adult life when you encounter setbacks at work or in family life. The teddy bear was moreover legitimate for boys too. Girls already had dolls to hug. With a teddy bear at one's side any Victorian empire-builder could stand firm and unmoved when the wind blew.

We can thus see how advertisements not just reproduce culture but also produce it, or rather how that class of people that Mike Featherstone (1994) calls "symbol producers" skilfully capture our dreams and give them a certain shape – one of an infinite number of possibilities, to which we direct our desire. Why teddy bears and not donkeys, pigs, or camels, which were also to be found in Margarete Steiff's collection? Ask the marketers and their skill in "listening to the market". Stephen Kline describes how "my Little Pony" was created after American surveys of what girls think of before they fall asleep, dreams that were realized in the form of small, pastel-coloured plastic ponies with long, combable manes and tails. In other words, the girlish longing to have a horse of one's own to look after was given a specific form, which simultaneously excluded all others, and this form perhaps says more about the inside of a marketer's head and about our cultural stereotypes about girls, about male and female, and not very much about the inside of a little girl's head before she falls asleep.

Advertisements thus give us models for how we should act, how we should think, what we should own. Although there are other models, they give us suggestions which are mixed and matched with all the force of commercial culture. Advertisements and other types of archival material are thus not just "innocent" reflections of their time, but also to a great extent help to create modern man and to change children's identities in today's post-modern society.

The Mythologization of Children

Further examples may be given of the significance of a historical perspective in the study of the commercialization of childhood. Today we see teddy bears everywhere. In advertisements for baby food, toothbrushes, and high chairs, as trendy accessories in furniture stores, as decoration on everything from mugs and wallpaper to shirts and underpants. The path of the teddy bear from the nursery to the shirt collar can only be explained in historical perspective, for example, through the gradual mythologization described by Roland Barthes (1970).

A myth is created, according to Barthes, when a representation, an "image" – the Swedish flag in a letterhead, for instance – is used to represent something completely different from the piece of blue and yellow cloth in itself, such as "Swedishness" or "nationalism". In the same way, the teddy bear as a myth has been constructed by means of several layers of meaning and symbolic recharges. With a rising degree of abstraction, the teddy bear has come to represent, for example, children, childhood, security. In the symbolic world, the myth of the teddy bear in addition interacts with other myths to build up an image of innocence, playfulness, goodness, and so on. An advertisement like that

Fig. 3. What is the teddy bear doing beside the packet of infant formula? Perhaps it is trying to tell us that we give our children a real childhood when we buy Findus wholemeal formula.

used by Findus to sell its infant formula – an advertisement that is geared to parents, not children – can only be understood in connection with the ability of the teddy bear figure to trigger a complete battery of associations and to convince parents that they are giving their children a "real" childhood by buying Findus's wholemeal formula.

Part of the explanation for the design of advertisements can also be found in the encounter of the global, or at least transnational, meanings with the national ones. As Hannerz and Löfgren (1992) have rightly pointed out, there has been a special relationship between market, state, and popular movements in Sweden, as a result of which commercialism has been integrated in a special way and charged with special symbols. An example that we have found in our work on the anthology is that the hedonistic message of the American toy industry – "Make your child's day a happy one, buy a toy" – finds it difficult to gain full acceptance among Swedish parents. Instead, it seems to be more important to convince hesitant Swedish parents of all social classes that the toys have an educational value; this indicates the special role played by state experts in Sweden, in competition with the market's symbol producers.

Pathetic Parents and Crafty Children

We assume that commercial culture has changed children's conditions in such a profound way that it also affects the most intimate relations and the sense of who one is. In our work with *Postmodern barndom* we detected many such areas where far-reaching changes had occurred. One example is the competence that children possess, their perception of time and place, and – not least of all – their relation to their parents. We shall round off this article by looking more closely at the latter.

In *Postmodern barndom*, both Linda Mauthe and Lotta Edin examine how advertising now bypasses the parents and appeals directly to the children, and how parents are portrayed in advertisements as twits who are easily outwitted and humiliated by their children. This development is obvious in Mauthe's analysis of forty years of advertisements in Swedish Disney comics, in which parents are gradually reduced from dependable, caring adults to powerless tools for the children's consumption. In the 1950s, parents were depicted as sensible adults buying bactericides and helping their children to write the address on the envelope. In the 1980s and 1990s, the children are the active subjects, highly aware consumers, who are expected to be able to look after themselves and take advantage of what the market has to offer, for example, to "take Mum and Dad to EuroDisney in Paris". In a competition organized by a Swedish sweet manufacturer, a child could even win an adult as a prize, the comedian Stellan Sundahl, who would be delivered to the winner along with a supply of sweets. "With his clever jokes, hilarious stories, and crazy pranks, he will make your day a birthday to remember." The roles are reversed: the adult is crazy and irresponsible, the child is the sensible and perhaps critical consumer.

Ellen Seiter (1993) describes the stereotyped presentation of adults in American television commercials aimed at children. White men are either conscientious workers or boring parents. Black men stand for the bodily or sensual aspects to do with sport or music. In advertisements for children, the attraction of the product often lies in the fact that it is the opposite of the adult world. The adults are the constant losers, those who vainly try to deprive the children of the pleasures of life, in the form of sweets and snacks. The point of the advertisements is often that an adult is exposed as stupid, false, or childish.

One could claim with Seiter that this is a clever way to design advertisements for children, to make them laugh and buy more. This in itself need not say very much about relations in the real world. It is no doubt possible to trace this mockery of the adult world further back in time in children's media. In *Postmodern barndom* Anne Simu and Lena Åkerman present a study of a children's television programme, *Fem myror är fler än fyra elefanter*, a Swedish variant of *Sesame Street*. They show how Brasse Brännström played the role of a shrewd and crafty child who often outwitted the adults in the form of the motherly Eva Remaeus and the schoolmasterly Magnus Härenstam. From our own childhood we remember a scatterbrained inventor father in Edith Unnerstedt's book *Kastrullresan (The Saucepan Journey)*, and Astrid Lindgren undoubtedly let Pippi Longstocking make fun of the adult world. Yet the moral panic that Pippi Longstocking provoked shows how unique and daring her mockery of the adult world was. This mockery has been multiplied to such an extent in the 1990s in advertisements and commercial television for children that it does not upset anyone or cause the slightest moral panic. In fact, it leaves the adult world unmoved, which might suggest that something rather radical has happened in relations between parents and children. In any case, it was not parents that Pippi made fun of; it was rather the pompous representatives of authority, such as policemen and superintendents of children's homes. Tommy and Annika's parents, like Pippi's own father and mother, were portrayed as good, worth all respect, and with an unquestioned authority, in a way that is increasingly uncommon in children's television nowadays.

The Family in Front of the Television

Even more thought-provoking are the images of parents that we see in television series which a re not primarily geared to children, being more family series. These abound in prim mothers and scatterbrained fathers who can hardly take a step without falling over. A clear example is the 1996 advent calendar, a series of television programmes leading up to Christmas; here the mother was a rational perfectionist and the father a failed inventor who made all the television sets in Sweden spark. Another example is the popular Swedish sitcom *Svensson, Svensson*. The series is about a "typical" Swedish family with two children, living in a suburban terrace house, and their everyday problems. The father constantly makes unsuccessful attempts to maintain his masculinity and family authority, accompanied by the sarcastic comments of the mother, a bank executive. Examples from outside Sweden are *The Wonder Years* and *The Simpsons*. Where do all the daft fathers and all the cheerless, priggish mothers come from? A historical perspective would presumably show that this phenomenon is nothing new either. It has gradually emerged and has been accentuated. One of the family favourites of the 1980s was *Cosby*, in which the two parents – he a doctor, she a psychologist – smoothly solved all the problems that arose in the large, rowdy family. *Cosby* is more than anything else a popular form of advice on child-rearing. From our own childhood we remember *Father Knows Best* and western series like *Little House on the Prairie* and *Bonanza*, in which the adults were always wise and understanding and the fathers were the true heroes.

According to viewing figures for 1996, *Svensson, Svensson* was the most popular programme in Sweden, with a maximum of 3.4 million viewers on an ordinary Sunday evening (*Göteborgs-Posten* 24 Jan. 1997). What made so many Swedish people, both young and old, sit and watch Allan Svensson and his family? What did they laugh at? Themselves? Their own parents? Or at the typical Swede who usually goes under the name "Svensson"? Is it a distorting mirror in which certain familiar features are grotesquely exaggerated? Or is it a contrasting picture which allows people to say, "At least I'm not like that"? Or could it be a dream image: "Imagine having the nerve to behave like that just once!"? And who laughs at it? Is it the children and the young parents who laugh at their own parents' failures? Is it the middle-aged generation's parody of disintegrating parental authority? Or is it the media makers' ironic commentary on their own parenthood?

Is the success of *Svensson, Svensson* due to the fact that the series has something more to say over and above the opportunities for laughter and identification that the characters in the series provide? Is it in fact a study of the modern problems of the parental role, and particularly the father's role? Does it test new ways to be a child in the family? The smart son in the family often outwits the adults, just as in the advertisements aimed at children, as a mixture of the traditional naughty boy and the boy genius (Seiter 1993:126). The boy genius is a new character in the commercial media, the only one for whom intellectual and verbal skills are highly valued, according to Seiter. He is a clever type who is cool in an individualistic way, far from the image of the traditional bespectacled nerd. Is this perhaps the revenge of the computer boys?

Television researchers, such as David Morley (1986), have stressed how the family is "constructed" in television series, but also by the real family in the social situation that watching television constitutes. Different families have different viewing styles, and a family can arrive at a shared understanding of how to perceive programmes and characters, an understanding that differs from that of other families. Morley's studies also show that the father in the viewing situation often adopts a playful role towards the children, while the mother has a more supervisory function. Perhaps it is primarily the family in the viewing situation that is parodied in *Svensson, Svensson*. Maybe family television viewing plays yet another role: cuddling up in the sofa in front of the television is perhaps the only chance that families have to sit close together. Morley argues that television viewing is the only activity in which this snuggling is really permitted between adults and children or between men and women – an act of intimacy, solidarity, and family togetherness. This enhances the significance of what happens both on the television screen and in front of it.

Fig. 4. When they use the modern media, children quickly become experts in the "new literacy", which brings a better eye for visual impressions and a greater ability to acquire simultaneous information.

New Competences

Do media discourses about pathetic parents and crafty children have a counterpart in reality? Most people can no doubt confirm that a great deal has changed in inter-generation relations in just a few generations. The self-evident authority once enjoyed by the schoolteacher and the father has been dissolved. Today schoolchildren can force through their demand that they too – and not just the teachers – should be allowed to eat biscuits during the school breaks, in the name of fairness. In the home it is often the children who urge a change to environment-friendly detergent and sorting of waste. Smoking parents may find it difficult to persist in their vice when they are confronted with the well-formulated arguments and severe sanctions of the children's anti-smoking campaigns. Children not only know more than adults in many fields, they also have the ability to argue for their views, showing their increased communicative competence.

When changes occur so quickly nowadays from one generation to the next, and the parents are no longer those who know best and have the answers to all the questions, it is natural for children to turn to their coevals to learn how to act in life. Nowadays, with rapid staff turnover in kindergartens and schools, with divorces and single parents with frequent changes of partner, it is perhaps a child's friends and not the parents that represent continuity.

Another example of something that never ceases to amaze parents is how easy it is for children to learn to use computers. It is not long after the PC is installed at home that the parents need the help of the son or daughter, who have experimented and learned things that the adult cannot find in the thick manuals. It is characteristic that a three-year-old girl who still cannot read, but who has sat playing with a drawing program and become skilled in clicking her way through the dialogue windows, can tell astonished visitors that "it's mostly

Daddy and me that use the computer, Mummy doesn't know so much, but she tries a bit".

It appears as if our information society in which pictures are so important requires new competences. To establish connections and understanding in the huge flow of simultaneous information, especially visual information, one must be able to grasp, interpret, and act quickly. One needs skills in reading pictures and learning the digital language, acquiring a coherent picture of what may seem to the untrained eye to be a mass of disconnected fragments. This new type of literacy is what children and young people practise when they zap between channels, read advertisements, and play computer games (Ziehe 1992). In contrast to the printed word, computer games are built up of interactive picture worlds. Unlike a book, one does not follow a set course from beginning to end; you can choose your own way through the virtual landscape. It is your choice, and you must accept responsibility for it. You never know what is waiting round the corner; someone can sneak up from behind at any moment. You have to be attentive in every direction, ever-prepared to act (Johansson 1996).

In the same way as with other language acquisition, it is the children who learn easiest and quickest, while adults will always speak it with a foreign accent. It is easy to see a parallel with the family that moves abroad and the children are the first to learn the language and culture of the new country, having to act as an intermediary for the parents.

"Post-modern" Technology

The example of the three-year-old girl is far from unique. The new adult–child relationship stands out with particular clarity when one looks at how adults and children relate to computer technology, a world in which adults are generally more cautious, showing greater respect for the computer, sticking to one or just a few programs which they more or less master. The typical attitude of the child, on the other hand, is inquisitive, testing, playful, and irreverent.

One can see in many ways how the computer fits into modern society, in which large quantities of information have to be handled quickly, in which priority is attached to flexibility in working life, where quick and long-distance communication is essential. In the post-modern era, when the grand narratives have been abandoned and life is characterized by fragmentation, a tourist existence (Bauman 1993), transcended boundaries, and a seemingly infinite number of options, the computer and the Internet afford the possibility of leaving the confines of everyday life and surfing in cyberspace. This in turn further reinforces these post-modern tendencies.

In the same way, we can see how the changed relationship between children and adults is supported by computer technology. It is not just that parents and teachers have to ask the children for help when they want to use the computer; the adults' control of the children is reduced. It is impossible to keep track of what the children download from the Internet, and they quickly learn how to hide their documents on the hard disk, safe from the eyes of curious adults. Yet it is not just children who appear more adult; the computer also gives adults an outlet for their more childish tendencies, as people know who have sat for hours – perhaps to their own amazement – wasting time with some computer game. Unlike children, however, adults have a tendency to stick to one game to which they constantly return, often a simple game that does not require any great intellectual effort. The children notice this and comment on it: "Daddy usually plays with a boat sailing on the sea and there's a lot of shooting" or "Mummy's always sitting playing patience". It is particularly bad, of course, when the adult is ashamed of his addiction to computer games and plays them furtively. One girl could tell about her father who would sit down at the computer to work and then, when she had left the room, she could hear the little tune from his favourite game. There is scope here for all kinds of attitudes on the part of the children, from scorn to gentle indulgence.

The Merger of Childish and Adult Behaviour

In the general discourse, in both popular science and serious research, we often glimpse pictures of young people who do not enter the adult role in the same way as previous generations did. Thomas Ziehe speaks in positive terms about a "normalization", in which the artificial boundaries which, in his view, modernity set up between adults and children, are now disappearing, and childhood is once again attaining its normal status as a part of adult culture. Others view this normalization as rather more problematic. The Italian sociologist Alberto Melucci (1992), for example, sees the dissolution of routinized transitions between different phases of life as a great danger for the process of becoming an adult. Perhaps we will have a society of eternal children with no responsible adults. Robert Bly, in his latest book *The Sibling Society* (1996), argues that adults are not just more immature than they were in the past; they have even been "infantilized" and thus lost the ability to bring up the next generation. He blames commercialism, which has had the effect that our rational brain, "the new mammalian brain" cannot curb the more primitive parts of the brain, "the reptilian brain" and "the old mammalian brain" but is flooded by hedonistic desire, sloth, and lust.

On the basis of the examples cited here, it seems as if the generational change is about something more complex than the normalization of which Ziehe speaks and the infantilization that Melucci and Bly fear. Perhaps we may look at it as increased interplay between "childish" and "adult", which are not so closely attached to specific age groups but instead have begun to flow freely between different generations. This can be seen in schoolboys who start computer companies and in grandmothers who dress as youthfully as their grandchildren. We see adults in television shows building towers out of beer crates and competing to see who can burst most balloons in a minute, and we see children who start national collections to save the rainforest.

The different interpretations may be seen as an attempt to read the signs of the times, signs which find fairly unambiguous expression in the media. In the same way as the Steiff advertisement can function as a peephole into bygone ideas about children and childhood, today's media images of children and adults may function as lookout points in a study of changed relations between adults and children. Contemporary studies give us ethnologists a chance to combine pure cultural analysis with studies of the meanings that children and parents create in the television-viewing situation, of how their use of the media can function as veritable identity-building work in the consumption society. All this provides a fascinating basis for new ethnological research.

Translation: Alan Crozier

Notes

1. Parallel to, or perhaps even before the Steiff bear, the American teddy bear began to be produced and marketed at the turn of the century, using largely the same advertising language.

References

Barthes, Roland 1970: *Mytologier*. Lund: Bo Cavefors.

Bauman, Zygmunt 1993: *Postmodern etik*. Göteborg: Daidalos.

Bjurman, EvaLis 1981: *Barn och barn: Om barns olika vardag*. Lund: Liber.

Bly, Robert 1996: *Syskonsamhället*. Västerås: ICA bokförlag.

Bocock, Robert 1993: *Consumption*. London: Routledge.

Brembeck, Helene & Johansson, Barbro (eds.) 1996: *Postmodern barndom*. Göteborg: Etnologiska föreningen i Västsverige.

Featherstone, Mike 1994: *Kultur, kropp och konsumtion*. Kultursociologiska texter i urval av Fredrik Miegel och Thomas Johansson. Stockholm/Stehag: Symposion.

Frönes, Ivar (ed.) 1987: *Mediabarn: Barnet, bildene, ordene og teknologien*. Oslo: Gyldendal.

Göteborgs-Posten 24 Jan. 1997: Svenska TV-program populärast i folkhemmet.

Hadenius, Patrik 1995: Full fart framåt. *Tur & Retur* 8.

Hannerz, Ulf, & Löfgren, Orvar 1992: Nationen i den globala byn. *Kulturella perspektiv* 1.

Johansson, Barbro 1996: Virtuella lekkamrater. *Kulturella perspektiv* 4/96.

Kildegaard Hansen, Bjarne 1987: Barneværelsets kulturhistorie: Den inbygde kontrol. In: Sigurd Berntzen & Brit Berggreen (eds.): *Barns sociale verden*. Oslo: Gyldendal Norsk forlag.

Kline, Stephen 1993: *Out of the Garden: Toys and Children's Culture in the Age of TV Marketing*. London/New York: Verso.
Löfgren, Orvar 1990: Huvudentréer och köksingångar i kulturstudiet. In: Henrik Horstbøll & Henrik Kaare Nielsen (eds.): *Delkulturer*. Aarhus Universitetsforlag.
Löfgren, Orvar 1992: Mitt liv som konsument: Livshistoria som forskningsstrategi och analysmaterial. In: Christoffer Tigerstedt, J. P. Roos & Anni Vilkko: *Självbiografi, kultur, liv: Levnadshistoriska studier inom human- och samhällsvetenskap*. Stockholm/Stehag: Symposion.
Löfgren, Orvar 1993: Swedish Modern: Konsten att nationalisera konsumtion och estetik. *Kulturstudier* 17. Aarhus universitet: Center for Kulturforskning.
Löfgren, Orvar 1996: Konsumtion som vardaglig praktik och ideologiskt slagfält. *Socialvetenskaplig tidskrift* 1–2/96.
Melucci, Alberto 1992: Youth Silence and Voice: Selfhood and Commitment in Everyday Experience of Adolescents. In: Johan Fornäs & Göran Bolin (eds.): *Moves in Modernity*. Stockholm: Almqvist & Wiksell International.
Morley, David 1986: *Family Television: Cultural Power and Domestic Leisure*. London and New York: Routledge.
Rönnberg, Margareta 1987: Lekeskjermen i mediaverdenen: Om TV som en form for lek. In: Ivar Frönes (ed.): *Mediabarn: Barnet, bildene, ordene og teknologien*. Oslo: Gyldendal.
Seiter, Ellen 1993: *Sold Separately: Parents and Children in Consumer Culture*. New Brunswick, New Jersey: Rutgers University Press.
Ziehe, Thomas 1992: Cultural Modernity and Individualization. In: Johan Fornäs & Göran Bolin (eds.): *Moves in Modernity*. Stockholm: Almqvist & Wiksell International.
Ziehe, Thomas 1993: *Kulturanalyser*. Stockholm/Stehag: Symposion.

Killing in the Name of the Lord

Cases and Reflections Regarding Reli-Criminality in the Western World

Jojada Verrips

Verrips, Jojada 1997: Killing in the Name of the Lord. Cases and Reflections Regarding Reli-Criminality in the Western World. – Ethnologia Europaea 1997: 29–45.

In Christian circles the tendency exists to deny that the causes of manslaugther and homicide may be due to the existence of a biblically based frame of orientation – indeed, that frame teaches respect for other persons' lives. However, it is shown that the presence of such a frame may also lead to gruesome forms of manslaughter, usuallly represented by Christians as absolutely un-Christian, devilish, or heathen aberrations, worse than homicides committed out of pure hatred, aggression, or self-defence. The purpose of this article is, first, to present a typology of biblically inspired fatal crimes (or 'reli-crimes') as they occurred in the last two centuries in Europe, and, second, to present an interpretation of the relationship between religious imagination and representation on the one hand and atrocious forms of physical violence towards fellow human beings on the other.

Professor Jojada Verrips, Anthropological-Sociological Center, University of Amsterdam, Oudezijds Achterburgwal 185, NL–1012 DK Amsterdam, The Netherlands.

Introduction[1]

'It is not the violence of the Westerner that has to be explained, but its combination with such a peace-loving religion as Christianity,' wrote sociologist of religion Ter Borg at the end of 1994 in a Dutch Newspaper (*Trouw* d.d. 17 December 1994). According to him this violence is an unrecognized paradoxical effect of Christianity: '[B]y prohibiting violence and even sacrifice, Christianity [as a matter of fact] unchained the violence of Christians.' This is an interesting though somewhat simplistic (Girardian) vision. Not only does it rest on the questionable assumption that every Westerner is Christian, but it also implies that the Christian taboo on physical violence (*vide* the sixth commandment) in general and on violent sacrifices in particular would generate this kind of violence. When Christians kill, Ter Borg seems to argue, they do so because of these prohibitions. If this is correct, it would certainly have been better if Moses had not come down from the mountain with the Ten Commandments. The author of the *Heidelberger Catechismus* wasted his time composing it, and if priests and preachers had left all references to the sixth commandment out of their sermons, then less or even no killing and murdering would have taken place. I think that there is much more to say about the relation – a topic that has already been studied by many scholars[2] – between Christian religion and physical violence practiced by its adherents.

In this paper I will try to shed some light on that intriguing relationship by presenting and analyzing what I once labelled 'reli-murders' (Verrips 1991). A reli-murder is a 'murder inspired by religious motives' in the sense that 'the committing of homicide or heavy physical abuse resulting in the death [of the victim(s)] by one or more persons who act under the influence of delusions in which religious moments are predominant' (Plokker 1948:147). By this definition one could consider a human sacrifice to a god to be a kind of particular reli-murder.

This, of course, is an outsider's view, for those who make such a sacrifice would not call it murder at all, but, for example, a very precious 'gift' to a deity. Though I realize that my definition does not do justice to the fact that committers of reli-murders may be totally convinced that they correctly interpret and implement their religion and therefore are not murderers at all, I still consider this act of religious loyalty to be murder. That it is not easy to decide what one can define as a 'crime' inspired by 'a religious belief system' is extensively shown by Lanning (1992:117/18). What X will characterize as an absolute misinterpretation of a belief system and as a crime may viewed by Y as a completely correct interpretation of the same system and as a benefit to a person or even to humanity.

In Christian circles the tendency exists to attribute manslaughter and homicide not to a biblically based (ethical) frame of orientation – after all, that frame teaches respect for other persons' lives – but rather to its absence. Because it is not there, so one reasons, it may happen that a person loses his self-control in a fit of extreme anger, jealousy, greediness, etc., and takes a person's life. However, that a biblically based frame of orientation also may lead to gruesome forms of manslaughter is mostly denied or else represented as an absolutely un-Christian, devilish, or even heathen aberration worse than homicide committed out of pure hatred, aggression, or self-defense. One comes across such a representation in the case of the killing of a farmhand in the Dutch village of Appeltern at the beginning of this century who was perceived by his murderer, a fanatical orthodox Protestant farmer, as a devil that should be crushed in order to bring the Lord's Kingdom closer. Abraham Kuyper, the founder of the *Gereformeerde Kerk* in the Netherlands, ascribed this homicide to: '[H]eathen customs that contrary to God's word partly remained alive in some regions of our country' (Van Belzen 1996:37).

Some years ago I developed a tentative typology of religiously inspired fatal crimes as they happened to occur – luckily infrequently but nevertheless with a certain regularity – in Western Europe and the USA (Verrips 1991). The purpose of that exercise was to create some order in the rather confusing amount of data and cases and by doing so to reach more insight into reli-criminality. I tried to make sense of differences in the background and nature of reli-murders and to estimate the probability of their disappearance. However, in the meantime several new cases have occurred. Though I am still convinced that my typology holds water, my ideas with regard to particular reli-murders underwent some elaboration. What I therefore intend to do in this paper is (1) to present and illustrate my typology of reli-criminality and (2) to sketch my latest ideas with regard to this fascinating phenomenon. It is my hope that our insight into the relation between religion (or religious imagination and representation) and physical violence will be thus deepened.

A Typology of Reli-murders

In the movie *The First Power*, directed by Robert Resnikoff, a detective specialized in tracing serial killers catches a ruthless murderer who used to carve five-pointed stars in the bodies of his victims. Although this satanic criminal has been executed, he returns in a miraculous way. 'Only a nun specialized in mystical skills is able to bring relief. She gives the detective a crucifix that contains a dagger. By stabbing the Devil in the heart he can stop him from doing his evil works' (*NRC HB* d.d. 4 October 1990). If one thinks that one is confronted here with just a figment of the imagination or a kind of crime that never takes place in reality, then one is really mistaken. For in this film two types of reli-murder occur that every now and then also occur in reality, i.e., (1) killing to please Satan ('sacrifice to Satan') and (2) killing somebody because he or she is deemed to be or to be associated with the Devil. The second type can be subdivided into three (sometimes overlapping) subtypes: killing a person, because one thinks he or she is (a) a satellite of demons and/or the Devil ('execution of witches'), (b) possessed by the Devil or devils ('exorcism murder'), and (c) the Devil himself ('Devil's murder').

Next to the two main types one can discern a

third, i.e., killing somebody because one thinks that it is necessary to make a sacrifice to God in accord with a biblical example. This type can be divided in two genres that I want to label (a) the 'Abrahams sacrifice' and (b) the 'crucifixion.' In the next sections I will illustrate these types and subtypes with case material.[3]

'Sacrifice to Satan'

The idea that certain people are in league with the Devil and commit all sorts of evil in his name, for example, bringing human sacrifices to honor him, is not only very old (cf. Cohn 1975), but still very much alive (cf. Sakheim & Devine 1992; La Fontaine 1992). This appears from the fact that in the last decades more and more people and institutions in the USA as well as several European countries not only report the occurrence of ritual child abuse, but even the ritual sacrifice of children by the members of a sect of Satan with branches all over the world. Very often their reports are based on fantastic stories told by children to their parents. They say, for example, that they have been enticed by strangers, sometimes dressed in clown costumes, who forced them to be present at and even to participate in the gruesome ritual of sacrificing age-mates. Nice illustrations of such 'eye-witness accounts' are the horror stories told by some of the kids involved in the sensational Oude Pekela case in the Netherlands a few years ago. In the meantime all sorts of specialists have done research on the empirical basis of the persistent and widespread rumors with regard to the ritual killing of children in order to please the Prince of Darkness. It is striking, however, that these specialists often had to conclude that there is no convincing evidence of large-scale ritual abuse of children and adults sometimes ending in their death. Yet especially in the last three decades, a few horrific cases of what I call 'sacrifice to Satan' took place. A well-known and gruesome example is the Tate-LaBianca-killings of 1969 in Los Angeles committed by the Manson Family (cf. Bugliosi & Gentry 1974). Apart from the USA (see, for example, Nash 1992:106 for the case of Joseph Cantero) there are also cases of 'sacrifices to Satan' reported for Hungary (cf. *Le Nouvel Observateur* d.d. 20 – 26 December 1990) and Germany. In a section of his book with the sensational title 'Blutopfer auf Satans Altar' Wiesendanger writes:

> Mitte Oktober 1987 saßen René (17) und Elke (15), Mitglieder der Lüdinghauser Teufelsgruppe 'Die Luzifikaner,' vor dem Landgericht Münster wegens Totschlags auf der Anklagebank: Am 15. Mai hatten sie sich mit Gruppenmitglied Anja (15) im Wald verabredet – zu ihrem gemeinsamen Todestag, 'um in Luzifers Reich einzugehen.' Als erste kam Anja dran: René und Elke schnitten ihr Hals und Pulsadern auf. Von ihren Schreien wachgerüttelt, rannten sie davon – Anja verblutete' (1995:32).

Wiesendanger also presents a number of cases where predominantly young people tried to 'sacrifice' themselves or peers to Satan, and others where they really achieved their aim. According to him it is important to realize, however, that these horrendous acts frequently called 'rituelle Opferungen' have not always owed to satanic motives alone. But I would stress that these motives were important and that one can not properly understand the crimes in question without taking them into consideration.[4]

'Murder of Witches'

Upon hearing the term 'murder of witches' many will immediately think of the 15th, 16th, and 17th centuries, when in several West European societies mostly women – often after torture – were burnt at the stake because they were thought to maintain real relations with demonic beings, especially God's dark antipode, the Devil, but less of the following centuries, especially the 20th.[5] Though one is prepared to accept that belief in witches and witchcraft persisted for a long time and in some places still does, one probably would be astonished to hear that cases of killing witches or attempts to do so have been occurring up until now.[6] Yet these cases took place, although – luckily – on a very modest scale. In the work of the German criminologist Hellwig, who developed a great interest in criminal acts partly originating in religious and so-called superstitious beliefs, one finds several examples of what I call 'murder of witches.' 'Mordtaten aus Hexenglauben,' as he writes (Hellwig 1908b:16), 'sind häufiger als man annehmen sollte,' and then he presents a long list of this kind of murder as they occurred all over Europe from the 19th century onwards. A very notorious case presented itself in 1896 in Germany.

In der Nacht vom 6. zum 7. Juli 1896 wurde die Witwe Euphrosine Gerber geborene Lösch in dem Dorfe Forchheim bei Endingen erwürgt. Der Verdacht der Täterschaft lenkte sich sofort auf den am 30. November 1875 geborenen ledigen, katholischen Landwirt Franz Xaver Werneth, dessen Großmutter väterlicherseits eine Schwester der Ermordeten gewesen war. Es war im ganzen Dorf bekannt, daß Franz Xaver Werneth und seine Angehörigen die Ermordete für eine äußerst boshafte Hexe hielten, der sie allerlei Unglück in Haus und Hof, ganz besonders aber die Epilepsie des Franz Xaver Werneth und die auf hysterischer Grundlage beruhende angebliche 'Besessenheit' seiner Tante Sibylla zuschrieben (Hellwig 1909:173).

In court the accused declared that he had to kill his aunt in order to get peace. God would not at all be angry with him because killing a harmful witch was something totally different 'als wenn einer den anderen aus Luxus totschlage' (Hellwig 1908b:16). The man was sentenced to ten years imprisonment.

Though there is evidence that 'murders of witches' took place elsewhere in Europe at the beginning of this century (cf. Hellwig 1908b), I did not come across clear-cut cases for the Netherlands. However, recently there was a court case that illustrates that belief in witchcraft in connection with threatening or even killing a person is not totally absent.[7] In 1988 the following remarkable message could be read in a Dutch newspaper:

Man is sentenced to five years for strangling his wife. Utrecht (ANP) – Last Tuesday O.A., (51) from Utrecht was sentenced by the court of Utrecht to five years imprisonment. October last year the man left his 22-year-old wife whom he had strangled in a ditch alongside the road in Utrecht. A. told the judge that his wife had been 'bewitched' (*Volkskrant* d.d. 6 April 1988).

Though in this case, about which I unfortunately could not collect more material, no 'witch' was involved but only a 'bewitched' woman, I present it in order to demonstrate that belief in witchcraft is still capable of inspiring persons to kill a human being.[8]

It may be possible that the murderer intended to say not so much that his wife was 'bewitched' as that she was 'possessed (by the Devil).' If this is correct, his crime would be an illustration of the next subtype.

'Exorcism Murder'

The fact that the special office of exorcist in the Roman Catholic Church no longer exists does not mean that within this church exorcism takes place no longer. Priests are still allowed to cast out demons and devils when they deem it necessary. In such cases they are bound by strict rules and not allowed to exorcise unless they have permission from their bishop. The same holds true for the Anglican Church. In Protestant churches, however, the ritual expulsion of the Devil or devils is nonexistent.[9] The idea that people may be possessed by evil spirits that may then be driven out is prevalent in the New Testament. There one may find the origin of exorcism as it has been practiced through ages and as it still takes place in the Roman Catholic and Anglican as well as in the Pentecostal churches. Though the purpose of exorcism has always been positive to rid people of evil spirits that occupied their bodies it sometimes resulted in the death of the possessed. Maquart, for example, remarks:

Malgré la sévérité de l'Eglise à ce sujet, il faut regretter parfois chez certain prêtres adonnés à ce dangereux ministère, la pratique inconsidérée et imprudente de l'exorcisme (1948:328).

But not only fanatical priests have been guilty of practicing exorcism with fatal consequences, but also laypeople.[10] Though the number of cases since the end of the 19th century has not been large, which by the way holds true for all the reli-murders I deal with in this essay, the world has not been disenchanted to such an extent that they occur no longer. In order to illustrate this I will present a few spectacular recent examples.

In 1957 Jozef Stocker, an excommunicated priest, together with his lover Magdalena Kohler founded in Ringwil near Zürich a small sect that he baptized the 'International Family Community for the Benefit of Peace.' Both believed that the end of the world was near. Stocker tried to persuade credulous peasants to buy a place in his 'Noah's Ark' so that they could escape the crack of doom. Together with Magdalena he engaged in the 'education' of children and adolescents entrusted to them by naive parents. One of their pupils was the seventeen-year-old farmer's daughter Bernadette Hasler. According to the guiding couple she was possessed by the Devil and only exorcism would cure her. In the spring of 1966 Stocker, his sweetheart, and a few faithful followers began to treat Bernadette. The results were dramatic. She died as a consequence of their healing efforts, which showed almost no resemblance to the treatment of possessed persons that is permitted in the Roman Catholic Church.

Sie prügelten Bernadette täglich, liessen sie ihre eigenen Excremente essen, gossen eiskaltes Wasser über sie, sperrten sie ein, liessen sie 400 Seiten Selbstbeschimpfungen aufschreiben, schlugen sie buchstäblich zusammen. Bernadette hat es nicht überlebt. Sie starb nachts, Kerzen umstrahlten ihr Bett, Stocker predigte wirres Zeug: 'Sie hat sich selbst befriedigt... o haben wir sie wenigstens vor der Hölle retten können...' (*Bild am Sonntag* d.d. 28 February 1988; see also *Frankfurter Rundschau* d.d. 9 November 1988).

Stocker and Magdalena, who appeared before the court in Zürich only in 1969, were sentenced to ten years of imprisonment each, whereas their accomplices got lighter punishments (cf. *Het Parool* d.d. 5 February 1969). While nothing was heard of Stocker since, Magdalena Kohler once became front page news again a few years later. I will return to that.

Nine years later two Roman Catholic priests and the parents of a young girl had to appear in court at Aschaffenburg because they had committed a similar kind of crime as Stocker and Kohler.

Before the court of Aschaffenburg in Bayern the Middle Ages are revived these days. There is talk about devils who call themselves Lucifer, Kain, Judas, Nero, Hitler, and pastor Fleischmann. They had taken possession of the body and soul of the innocent girl Anneliese Michel from Klingenberg near the Main river. The six devils were expelled by two Catholic clergymen, but at the end of the 'exorcism' the girl was quite dead. She died of undernourishment (*Volkskrant* d.d. 6 April 1978 – transl. J.V.).

After a spectacular trial the four persons accused, who were absolutely convinced that they had done no harm, got a sentence of six months' probation for having caused the death of the girl (cf. *Volkskrant* d.d. 22 April 1978).[11]

Precisely twelve years after Anneliese Michel died in consequence of an exorcism, almost all Dutch newspapers reported that the police of Velp (a small town in the province of Gelderland) had arrested a local couple and a woman from Maassluis because they had burned a baby to death after trying in vain to cast out the demons that possessed it.

The burning of the baby...in the lavatory of the house of the couple in Velp was, according to police, the climax of an exorcism ritual that lasted 48 hours. Initially the father (30), the mother (27), and their friend (31) assaulted the baby with pillows and knives. Afterwards they poured alcohol, paint, and hydrochloric acid over the baby and set it on fire. The police speak of a ritual murder (*NRC HB* d.d. 1 July 1988).[12]

Because there are indications that the little victim was deemed to be the Devil himself, I will return to this case when treating 'Devil's murders.'[13]

Though the tragic event in Velp was front-page news, a few other cases that occurred shortly before and after it got almost no attention from journalists. However, there were two remarkable short items in the newspapers with regard to the type of killing I am dealing with here. On 29 January 1988 one could read the following:

Psychiatric confinement demanded for the stabbing of a woman in order to cast out the Devil. Groningen (ANP) – Before the court of Groningen public prosecutor M. Severein...demanded unconditional psychiatric confinement of a 28-year-old inhabitant of Groningen who committed homicide. The man is suspected of having killed his 37-years-old girlfriend on 8 August last year because he believed that she was possessed by the Devil. During the four months that he and the victim were involved, they regularly indulged in the exorcism of spirits. Just before the tragic event took place, the man became convinced that the Devil had taken possession of his girlfriend. In order to cast him out he stabbed her. The public prosecutor followed the psychiatric report, which says that L. suffers from paranoid psychosis and is of unsound mind. Verdict on 11 February (*Volkskrant* d.d. 29 January 1988).

In November, the newspapers reported a case against a German woman of 74 who was accused of having killed in February 1988 (together with her since deceased sister) a widow of 66 because they thought that she was possessed by Satan (cf. *Volkskrant* d.d. 9 November 1988). On 23 February a German newspaper published the following:

66-jährige zu Tode geschlagen. Singen. (dpa) – Einem ungewöhlichen Verbrechen, in dem nach den ersten Ermittlungen religiöser Wahn und jahrenlange Teufelsaustreibung die Hauptrolle spielten, ist jetzt in Singen (Kreis Konstanz) aufgedeckt worden. Wie die Konstanzer Staatsanwaltschaft und die Polizei gestern mitteilten, sind zwei 70 und 73 Jahre alte Frauen am 19. Februar verhaftet worden, weil sie eine 66-jährige Witwe jahrelang gefangen gehalten und zur 'Austreibung des Teufels' so geschlagen hatten, dass diese Anfang Februar an ihren Verletzungen gestorben war (cf. *Rhein-Sieg-Zeitung* d.d. 23 February 1988).

This case is interesting, because the main suspect was no one else but Magdalena Kohler whom we met before. In the 80s Magdalena, who after her early release from prison was expelled from Switzerland and settled in Singen, still believed that she was chosen by the Lord. She now claimed that the Madonna had appeared and told her to gather a family around herself, just as she had done before, in order to survive a coming catastrophe. Magdalena's victim had been a member of the sect founded by herself and Jozef Stocker. A unique case of recidivism! During the trial Magdalena's lawyer made the interesting remark that she had once again made a mistake 'nicht weil, sondern obwohl sie fromm war.' We can observe here that killing someone is not seen as the result of religious beliefs held by the offender, but rather as the consequence of something totally different, for example, a state of mental derangement or an attack of insanity that has no relation with these beliefs at all. That such attacks have a clear-cut connection with religion and can be seen as a kind of pathological implication seems to be toned down or even denied, especially by the experts, for example, psychiatrists and psychologists, who are recruited to make sense of such cases (cf. Van Meer 1988, Verrips 1988, Van Belzen 1996). By defining the state of mind of what I would call 'reli-delinquents' in technical jargon as, for example, *'ontoerekeningsvatbaarheid als gevolg van een paranoïde psychose veroorzaakt door schizofrenie'* ('mental incompetence as a consequence of a paranoid psychosis caused by schizophrenia') one conceals more than one clarifies about the pathological turn that the religious thinking of specific people can take under particular circumstances. Such labelling deprives us of a clear perspective on the logic of the offenses and on how that logic can originate from, for example, the Bible or theological treatises.[14] These writings may function as a source not only of orientation but also of disorientation such that people may become totally confused and fall into criminal behavior, though they would not admit it to be such. On the contrary, they often think that they did something to benefit a particular person or even humanity.[15] It is striking that journalists who write about such misdeeds often describe them as 'devilish.' For example, the two elderly sisters who exorcised the lady of 66 until she died were more than once characterized as 'die teuflischen Schwestern' just as their homicide was called 'teuflisch.' We are confronted here with the relative nature of what people experience as good or evil.

Also in the 90s a number of fatal exorcisms took place. In 1993, for example, two fortune-tellers in Spain who tried to exorcise a ten-year-old girl manhandled her in such a way that she died of her injuries (*VPRO-Gids* d.d. 19 May 1993). And in 1995 a child died in Canada after her grandmother had poured water in her throat in order to cast out the Devil who possessed her (*VPRO-Gids* d.d. 16 December 1995).[16]

The people who start an exorcism do not intend to kill a possessed person. On the contrary, they want to deliver him or her from tormenting spirits. However, if these demons do not go away, the exorcists sometimes intensify their healing efforts in such a way that the possessed succumbs. In the beginning they still distinguish between the possessed and his or her possessors, but as the ritual goes on because the demons will not leave the distinction may become sometimes so vague that the exorcists start thinking that the possessed *is* the Devil in person who must be destroyed. This dramatic development typically occurs when laymen undertake deliverance 'rituals' (*vide* the case of Magdalena Kohler). There exists smooth transition to the cases I shall treat now.[17]

'Devil's Murder'

Characteristic of this kind of reli-murder is that the victim is perceived not as possessed by the Devil but as the Devil in person. In the eyes of the murderers their victim is not somebody who suffers from demonic powers who took possession of his or her body, but is Satan himself whom they can expel only by radically destroying him. Sometimes, but not always, this destruction is preceded by a kind of exorcism. During this century several spectacular 'Devil's murders' took place in the Netherlands. The most sensational Dutch cases occurred in the village of Appeltern (1900), at sea aboard a lugger from Katwijk (1915), and in Weverwijk, a small hamlet near Meerkerk (1944).[18] Since they form prototypical cases I will briefly sketch each of them here.[19]

On the night of 2 to 3 February 1900, the ultra-orthodox Calvinist farmer Mettinus Scherff (also called Marius) smashed – in his farm-house and whilst his wife, five children, maidservant, and the girls Mina en Emma Levoir were present – the skull of his Roman Catholic farmhand Piet with a blowpipe because he thought him to be the Devil himself.[20] After this Marius fancied that he was the returned Jesus Christ, and he and his followers expected the coming of the millennium. Preceding the event various things had happened, for example, an effort of Marius to deliver Emma Levoir from dark forces. During this exorcism he ordered his servant

> to hold the chamberpot in order that Emma could spit the Devil into it. Marius then screwed up her eyes, hit her in the face, and asked: 'Do you feel that?' She answered: 'No.' What happened afterwards, she does not remember very well. She saw how Piet fell down, 'hit by God's hand.' Then the Devil came out of her mouth and eyes. She saw flames and heard roaring. She thinks that the Devil came out of her and took possession of Piet. At that moment she felt enlightened. She remembers how the slain body lay upon the floor and how it was treaded upon and beaten by Marius and the others... She also saw how Marius trampled on the corpse's chest till blood was flowing out of it. Afterwards she was very happy just like all the others who were present. She felt so well, so very well, for they had conquered the Devil. And they sang: Blessed be the Lord, the Devil has been slain! (Ruysch 1900:89).

The participants were never brought to court and sentenced. Though this case differs in several respects from the one in Velp I dealt with above, there is a remarkable resemblance.[21] In both cases the reli-delinquents started with an effort to cast out demons or the Devil but later grew convinced that the Prince of Darkness had materialized in a human being.[22]

Fifteen years after the reli-murder in Appeltern, the crew of the saillugger KW 171 from Katwijk literally and figuratively went adrift when an ultra-orthodox Calvinist sailor claimed that the world had ended. After having several visions, for example, of the New Jerusalem, he thought to recognize Satan in one of the crew members and ordered his death, whereupon the unlucky man was killed and thrown overboard. The next day the sailor and a companion cleft the skull of another hand because he also was considered to be a devil. Finally, a third devil was discovered aboard the lugger and also killed in a horrific way. After these murders the sailor ordered them to throw everything overboard since the crew needed nothing anymore. After the remaining fishermen had unrigged the ship, they lay down hoping soon to be in heaven, where they thought their fellow humans would already be. However, the rudderless wreck was noticed by the crew of a Norwegian merchantman who took the exhausted fishermen aboard and brought them to Grimsby. In this case also no prosecution followed because the men were deemed to be mentally incompetent when the killings took place.

In 1944 another sensational reli-murder occurred in the Netherlands, this time in an ultraorthodox Calvinist peasant family consisting of a father, mother, three daughters, and six sons living in a hamlet near Meerkerk. Religion and especially the question whether one belonged to God's chosen few formed the pivot on which everything hinged in this family. At the beginning of 1944 one of the sons was troubled by an unprecedented test of faith that lasted for hours and ended with prophecies. The end of the world was near, Satan who went roaring around would be crushed, Jesus would appear on the clouds, and the Kingdom of the Lord would come down to earth. Except for one son, everyone believed what the anguished man predicted. Hereafter life on the farm took an exceptional turn. The family neglected normal daily chores, hardly ate or drank any longer, stopped the clocks, and instead of sleeping sung and prayed. At a certain moment one of the family members came to the conclusion that the unbeliever in their midst was the Devil in person and that he had to be destroyed in order to speed up the coming of the Lord's Kingdom. Thereupon the man was killed in a horrendous way by his next of kin.[23] Again no prosecution followed because of the supposed mental incompetence of the actors.

Striking in this and similar cases[24] is that people imagine that someone is a devil or even Satan himself and that his destruction is a *conditio sine qua non* for deliverance from evil and a quiet life in this world or a new one to come. In the other two subtypes this idea is lacking. There seems to be no final reckoning with the Prince of Darkness and his accomplices, or at best a temporary one, and that is exactly what distinguishes these subtypes from the one I deal with in this section. Although the result in each case is the same, that is, the death of human beings, the ideas and motives which lead to it are different. However, in each case the deeds originate from the same source, namely a firm belief – well-founded in the Bible and time and time again confirmed by theologians – in the existence of the Devil and of his being active – directly or indirectly – in this world.

That the number of Christians who through that imagery become murderous has drastically diminished does not mean that this belief does not influence people any longer such that they kill innocent others. This became evident, for instance, in a poignant way in December 1994 when Margrit Müller (43) during an early mass at the St. Mary Church in Hamburg smashed the skull of Hedwig Buhr (72), whom she perceived to be a devilish competitor for a seat ('Sie war des Satans – sie sass auf meinem Platz' [*Bild* d.d. 15 December 1994]), with an axe. Since this case has different aspects that are important for developing deeper insight into the occurrence of 'Devil's murders,' I will sketch them here. Although Margrit Müller was originally Protestant, she made a pilgrimage to Lourdes with her sick mother three times. – In vain, for the old woman died in 1979. After that Margrit was not only seriously troubled by hallucinations, but also started hearing voices. This condition became worse after her relation with an ultra-orthodox Catholic man suddenly came to an end. Next to words of consolation she also got threats from what she called the 'Lourdes-Sau' ('Lourdes sow') or sexually perverted 'Satansnutte' ('Satan's whore'). Her skin would be ripped off and given as food to all kinds of carnivorous birds. Neither praying nor stays in clinics brought relief. Also her entry into the Roman Catholic Church did not silence the voices of the 'Lourdes-Sau' or the 'Satansnutte.' When she then got the message that she still had one task to accomplish, she decided to dispatch a Roman Catholic. She announced her mission in several letters, but in vain, for no one paid any attention to her horrific warnings (cf. *Stern* no. 28 1995). The specialists who treated Margrit Müller after her lugubrious homicide called her psychotic as seems to be the custom in cases like this. Earlier on I remarked that such a label can seriously impede better insight into the logic on which these cases are based and their origin in the Bible and theological treatises. In my conclusion I will come back to this case.

A striking phenomenon in the publications about 'Devil's murder' is that they are very often represented as a ritual offering or a sacrificial killing (cf., for example, Schotman 1946:34 and Van Rooy 1949:24), whilst the perpetrators almost never use that terminology. This does not mean, however, that it would be impossible to interpret the murders as sacrifices. I have done so at an earlier occasion (Verrips 1987), when – referring to Hubert & Mauss' [1898] famous theory on the nature and function of sacrifice – I tried to answer the question whether these murders would serve to reach a state of sacredness *or* to get rid of something polluting? I had to conclude that they served both these purposes, and that the pollution one wanted to get rid of had to do with sexuality experienced as sinful.[25]

Meanwhile, several reli-offenses took place that undoubtedly were motivated by a desire to make a sacrifice (in the sense of an offering to God).

The Killing of Others as Sacrifice

The 'Abraham's Sacrifice'

The Bible (especially the Old Testament) teems with passages about the sacrifice of human beings, for example, small children (cf. Dronkert 1955). Almost without exception it concerns acts committed by heathen idolaters that are disliked by the Lord and therefore sharply condemned. However, there happen to be cases where that condemnation does not occur. The best known example is Abraham who got the order from above to sacrifice his son Isaac, an order that was cancelled at the last moment. Time and time again this biblical story has inspired for committing fatal crimes, especially killing one's children, which I therefore call 'Abraham's sacrifices.'[26] In the works of Ideler one finds several of these tragic offenses described. An example:

In the county of Norfolk a tanner murdered his four children, the eldest only being four years of age. Three of them were killed by smashing their skull with a hammer, whilst the youngest, a little girl of ten weeks, was kept so long under water till she drowned. The tanner was convinced that in committing this heinous crime he served the Lord and he called the killing of his offspring an ABRAHAM's *sacrifice* (1851:211).

This type of crime also occurred in the Netherlands. A dramatic case is reported for Born in the province of Limburg. In 1917 a Roman Catholic woman there killed five of her seven children and severely wounded the other two as well as her husband. About the background of this stupefying act Van der Scheer says the following:

Zu Hause angelangt, kam ihr beim Kartoffelschälen – es war zur Zeit der Hochmesse – plötzlich die *Eingebung*, daß sie am Mittwoch 8 Personen töten müsse und daß damit gemeint seien ihr Mann und 7 Kinder. Sie widersetzte sich mit aller ihrer Kraft dieser Eingebung, um sich über das Schreckliche dieses innern Befehles, den sie als von Gott herrührend und vom dem Schutzengel als eingegeben betrachtete, hinwegzusetzen. Sie bat, dies Opfer nicht von ihr zu verlangen. Jedoch erinnerte sie sich, daß der Pastor vor einigen Wochen gepredigt hatte, daß jemand, der eine große Übeltat gegen seinen Willen begehe, keine Todsünde tue, und ferner suchte sie sich mit dem furchtbaren Gedanken dadurch zu versöhnen, daß sie an Abrahams Opfer dachte (1917:204).

What is striking in this case is that it concerns a woman who identified with a man, that is, Abraham. However, this is no unique phenomenon as we can learn, for example, from a case that occurred a few years later in a Calvinist milieu in the Veluwe, an orthodox region in the province of Gelderland. Though there are no explicit references to Abraham's sacrifice in this case and other traits appear that are lacking in the Born case, here we also meet a woman who 'bended' her gender and insisted – luckily in vain – upon sacrificing two children.[27]

Though I have looked for other examples of Abraham's sacrifices after the tragic incident in Born, I found none between 1917 and 1993, when a 42-year-old man from Hoek in the province of Zeeland was sentenced to six years of imprisonment for killing 'on purpose, with malice aforethought, and after calm deliberation' his two children. Before the court he asserted that he had received an order from the Lord to 'let them fall asleep' (*NRC HB* d.d. 31 July 1993). There are indications (for instance, passages in his farewell letter) that the father who in March 1996 in Assen (capital of the province of Drenthe) killed his three children and then committed suicide also acted on order of the Lord (*NRC HB* d.d. 20 March 1996). In any case together with his children he wanted to be reunited with his deceased wife whom he thought to be in heaven. The two cases mentioned belong to a series of childkillings in the Netherlands, which started in 1988 and of which five occurred in 1996. It would be worthwhile to find out if the killers in the other cases also got orders from the Lord or similar metaphysical instructions. One of the main motives for the killing of one's own children seems to be the desire to safeguard them against evil in this world, that cesspit of vice and impurity, and to let them go as pure as possible to heaven. Did not Jesus say, 'Let the children come to me?'[28]

Walter Schubart distinguishes four kinds of 'aberration and degeneration' of eroticism and religion, i.e. jealousy and fanaticism, erotic and religious nihilism, masochism, and sadism. In the context of this essay what he says about religious masochism is particularly relevant. In case of religion it may happen, Schubart argues, that an adoring love leads to an enormous aggrandizement of the adored one, i.c. God, on the one hand and an effacement of one's self on the other. And this may be a source of masochism or 'a form of degeneration of the adoring love for God' (1941:172). In the last resort this can imply self-destruction or suicide. 'In religion the masochistic urge to self-destruction often disguises itself as a desire to mortal martyrdom' (ibid.:173). We are confronted here with an extreme kind of mystic masochism that, according to Schubart, is one source of making sacrifices.

> And because human beings are the greatest that man can sacrifice, the masochistic character sanctifies human sacrifice as the worthiest form of worshipping God. He sacrifices human beings whom he loves and whose dying causes the contraction of his heart. Of the original emotional attitude of the sacrificer, of the dismaying experience of one's own paltriness, of the trembling before the face of the Lord, the patriarch Abraham is the classical example. A real sacrifice still implies that we love what we sacrifice and that we sacrifice exactly that which we by preference would most like to keep (read: our neighbour, our child, ourself) (ibid.:175).[29]

This brings me to the subtype of reli-criminality that I want to deal with now.

'The Crucifixion'

The general category 'killing a human being as a sacrifice' also includes another type of reli-murder, namely the 'crucifixion.' Here killing someone and committing suicide as a kind of offering are mixed up in a complex way. However, in killing and suicide Jesus' death on the cross functions as the 'model for.' In order to avoid making matters too complicated I will not deal here with cases of pure self-crucifixion, which occurred now and then in the last two centuries, but concentrate on what could be termed 'crucifixion in union.'[30] In such a case a man or woman imagines that he or she is Jesus Christ and succeeds in convincing his or her followers to nail him or her to a cross. The imitation of the suffering of Christ is pushed to the bitter end, so to speak.

An early case of this type of reli-delinquency took place in March 1823 in Wildenspuch (Switzerland). The main actress was the fanatical farmer's daughter Margaretha Peter. Together with a number of kindred spirits she had gathered in her parental home, she fought against devils and demons who had taken possession of her brother and sister. After the latter had been beaten to death at her instigation Margaretha requested her followers to crucify her first and to smash her skull afterwards in the idle hope – shared by her helpers – that she would be resurrected soon after (cf. Ideler 1851:205 – 10).[31]

An exceptional case I briefly want to mention here occurred in 1959 in Frankfurt. There the 64 year old shoemaker George Krausert, self-appointed leader of a small sect of religious fanatics who strongly identified with Jesus, committed suicide by hanging himself in order 'to give the world back its senses.' Shortly after a few of his disciples crucified his body to the wall of his sitting room.[32] Strictly speaking this case does not fit here, because Krausert's crucifixion took place only after he died, but it was so evidently inspired by the biblical model that I categorize it as 'crucifixion.' That the frequency of this kind of delict has been small in the last two centuries I find less important than the fact that it occurred at all. For its occurrence once again demonstrates that particular passages from the Bible may orient certain people in such a way that they become a danger to themselves and to people around them.[33] It concerns atrocious examples

> von der Suggestivkraft, die manche Partien des Alten und Neuen Testaments, besonders die Opferung Isaaks und der Sühnetod Christi auf empfängliche, vielfach pathologische Naturen auszuüben vermögen (Hellwig 1908a:186/87).

Because it would make my essay too long I cannot deal here with a type of murder that shows a remarkable family resemblance to the (sub)genres presented so far. I mean the lethal crimes evidently influenced or inspired by modern mythological discourses such as novels and movies. Like the 'palaeo-mythologically' inspired crimes, the 'neo-mythological' ones are indeed few, but they nevertheless occur with a certain regularity. It is striking that the 'disorienting' effect or lethal implication of old myths is usually underexposed whilst that of the new ones is greatly exaggerated (cf. Verrips 1995).

Concluding Remarks

In this contribution I have tried to present a tentative typology of reli-murders in the last two centuries in Europe and the USA. The creation of order in phenomena that at first sight make a puzzling and chaotic impression is a first step on the road toward a deeper understanding. A number of types and subtypes can be distinguished. One of the main distinguishing criteria is the biblical passages on which the killers based their thought and action, especially those dealing with the casting out or destruction of demons, devils, and Satan on the one hand and Abraham's sacrifice and Jesus' suffering and death at the cross on the other, often but not always in combination with eschatological sections. Elsewhere I argue (Verrips 1987) that the pathological use of biblical stories can be explained at least partly as a consequence of tremendous problems (especially in the realm of sexuality), that certain people are confronted with owing to their interpretation of other parts of the Bible or theological treatises. I will come back to this shortly. Here we encounter a shady side of Christianity that is too often neglected. It turns out to be a double-edged sword in the sense that it propagates nonviolence, but may stimulate certain people under specific circumstances to do exactly the opposite. The perpetrators I deal with did not want to do evil but wanted instead to do good. But in this regard there exists a difference between 'exorcism murders' and 'Devil's murders.' The former are a tragic result of a derailed ritual begun to end the suffering of an individual, whilst the latter concern crimes committed on behalf of mankind, for after crushing the Devil the Kingdom of the Lord is expected to come down to earth. A similar difference can be noticed between the 'Abraham's sacrifice' (as well as the 'sacrifice to Satan') and the 'crucifixion,' for the former also is an individual affair and the latter is for the benefit of humanity.

Moreover, it is striking that 'exorcism murders' generally take a less gruesome turn than 'Devil's murders.' In the first case the killings are seldom followed by efforts of the killers to radically destroy their victims. In order to better understand this conspicuous difference it seems important to note that 'exorcism murders' usually occur in Roman Catholic and Anglican circles, where rituals of deliverance are officially accepted, and that 'Devil's murders' are generally committed by ultra-orthodox Protestants, who are unfamiliar with these rituals. While Roman Catholics and Anglicans are taught that the Devil after having manifested himself in someone can be cast out, ultra-orthodox Protestants cannot resort to such a practice, for it is officially rejected. Is it possible for the former to 'domesticate' Satan and his henchmen, though this may get out of control, whereas the latter lack this option altogether and are left with little else but prayer and, if this does not work, waging a life-and-death struggle in order to literally destroy him. It seems that the relation between the divine status claimed by ultra-orthodox Protestant perpetrators of 'Devil's murders' and their horrendous crimes owes to their not being raised in a theological tradition that accepts exorcism. However, being socialized in such a tradition does not guarantee that excesses will not occur.

I think that the inability of Protestants to exorcise has to do with their conception of the relation between body and mind (spirit, soul) as it developed during and after the Reformation. Whilst Catholics acknowledged that alongside the spiritual the corporal was important in the religious realm, Protestants developed the view that the spirit dominates and the body serves. Catholics somatized the spiritual, and Protestants desomatized it (cf. Roper 1994:177).[34] According to Catholic doctrines the body, being the temple of the Holy Ghost, may and must be purified of pollution. According to orthodox Protestant doctrines it cannot be cleansed of evil (especially sexual lust). A willing spirit is often kept prisoner in bad, devilish flesh.[35] Because of the subordination of the body to the mind *and* the idea that the former is the source of drives and desires that are not bad in themselves but may be used in sinful ways, orthodox Protestants in default of a ritual able to clean the body of polluting evil are left with a problem. They can only *think* the body pure, for example, by projecting the sinfulness of their own onto another already killed or about to be killed and by expecting that they will be purified by the blood of this victim. Most Christians do this by thinking of Jesus and his grace-bringing death on the cross, but some lost souls do not and instead perceive the Devil in someone else whom they literally try to shatter. To kill the Devil in the shape of another person, who represents a sinful part of the self, can thus be seen as a sacrifice in order to get rid of evil radically and so to become a human being equalling God.[36] One may think that the case of Margrit Müller's 'Devil's murder' contradicts my argument, for as a Catholic she did not take resort to exorcism, but instead cleft – just like other Protestant killers of the Devil – the skull of somebody in whom she saw a kind of devil. However, if one realizes that Müller was raised a Protestant and only later converted to Roman Catholicism, her horrific crime becomes more understandable.[37] She did what one might expect of a Protestant who became totally possessed by his religion.

More abstractly, one could say that what is called 'devilish' is a metaphor for everything in an individual that is 'chaotic,' 'disturbing,' 'disorderly,' 'uncivilized,' 'wild,' in short his or her 'shady other side' that cannot be denied but has to be suppressed or even to be cast out in the interest of the continuation of the established order. As I point out, unlike Catholics orthodox Protestants subordinate the corporeal to the spiritual and ignore the possibility that devils and demons may take temporary possession of someone's body and so reject exorcism rituals. For that reason they do not know how to handle manifestations of this shady other side or puzzling otherness which, if not recognized as an essential part of the self, is often projected – as Lacan remarks – on someone else who then becomes an object of aggression (cf. Shapiro 1995:112). Tolerance implies the acceptance, at least to a certain degree, of what is 'disorderly,' 'different' or 'devilish' in one's own or another person's body, society and culture. And this is only possible if one is prepared to recognize and acknowledge what is 'disorderly,' 'different' or 'devilish' within one's own self. When Ter Borg states that the violence Christians may commit is a result of their prohibitions with regard to physical violence in general and violent sacrifice in particular, I cannot say this is completely irrelevant and incorrect. However, against the background of the material presented in this paper I think that his view is simplistic. For my argument clearly demonstrates that between these prohibitions and their dreadful 'trance-gressions' an intricate complex of diverse social and psychic processes is hidden that remains absolutely obscure if one accepts Ter Borg's Girardian viewpoint. In order to understand this complex one has to consider all sorts of biblical representations, theological doctrines, and religious rites based on them, as well as how this ensemble under specific conditions may be pathologically interpreted and violently put into practice. Studying the extreme cases presented here in which people evidently became possessed by their own religious beliefs and lost their respect for the physical integrity of others on whom they had projected their own unbearable and confusing otherness can be useful for developing deeper insights in the commission of violence by believers in palaeo- or neo-mythological stories. If these extreme cases deter, they probably do so not only because they are horrific but also because they fix our thoughts on the frailty of the civilized husk covering our wild core. 'We seem to move on a thin crust which may at any moment be rent by the subterranean forces slumbering below' (Frazer 1922:36).

Notes

1. I am grateful to Rod Aya for editing this article.
2. A recent example of such a study is the rather cynical one by the German theologian-sociologist Horst Herrmann, *Passion der Grausamkeit* (1994).
3. Because it would take too much space I will not deal in this paper with cases in which the leaders of religious groups stimulate their followers to: (a) mutilate their own bodies and the bodies of their children (as the leaders of the Russian Khlysty and Skoptzy did), (b) commit suicide (as Jim Jones the founder of Jonestown did in 1978, Luc Jouret of the Order of the Temple of the Sun did in 1994 and 1995, and as Marshall Applewhite of the cybersect Heaven's Gate did in 1997), and (c) to kill non-sect members (as Shoko Asahara the spiritual leader of the Aum Shinrikyo or Seekers of the Truth did in 1995). Strictly speaking, only the last phenomenon (c) falls in the general category of reli-murders. However, it is difficult to be strict, for in cases that at first sight appear to be religiously inspired collective suicides, 'ritual' murdering might still be involved (as is said of Luc Jouret's sect).
4. That one has to be very careful about calling the murderous activities of Satanists as ritual sacrifices can be illustrated by the case of Sandro Beyer. In 1993 this boy from Sondershausen (Thüringen) was killed by three members of a club of Satanists at a remote spot in a forest where they used to gather in order to perform particular rites. In the media this crime was almost immediately represented as a horrific example of a satanist sacrifice. However, convincing evidence that Sandro Beyer was really sacrificed to the Devil in the way sometimes described in satanist publications could not be found. There is every indication that the three boys who killed Sandro just wanted to get rid of him because he became too exacting and had threatened to tell tales about their satanic rites in the forest (cf. *Stern* d.d. 19 May 1993 and *Der Spiegel* d.d. 17 May 1993). Thus we are confronted here with a case of homicide that could not be properly understood without paying attention to satanism, but that nevertheless cannot count as a 'sacrifice to Satan.'
5. The Bible teems with passages in which sorcery is strongly forbidden (*vide,* for example, De Jong 1959:84). So one can read in *Exodus* (22:18): 'You shall not permit a sorceress to live,' and in *Revelation* (21:8): 'But as for the cowardly, the faithless, the polluted, as for murderers, fornicators, sorcerers, idolaters, and all liars, their lot shall be in the lake that burns with fire and sulphur, which is the second death.' See for a connection between sorcery and the Devil *Acts* (13:6 ff.).
6. In connection with the belief in witches and witchcraft I want to note the existence, especially in Great Britain, of generally small groups of people who consider themselves to be witches (cf., for instance, Luhrmann 1989 and Greenwood 1995).
7. For the second half of the 19th century several cases are known in which putative 'witches' were threatened with death and sometimes severely ill-treated. In the *Provinciale Drentsche & Asser Courant* d.d. 21 March 1873 one could, for instance, read: 'A family in Leksmond thought that their daughter was bewitched. Last Thursday a 30-year-old woman who was accused of the crime was called to the house. There was a great fire burning with a kettle hanging above it full of boiling water. She was summoned to bless the daughter or to lift her bewitchment. When the accused said that she did not have the power to do this, five persons attacked her and threatened to burn her in the kettle with boiling water. She was manhandled and only after she had screamed for some time that she was murdered the door was opened. The ill-treated [woman] walked bleeding all over to the mayor.' I am grateful to

Willem de Blécourt who drew my attention to this case.

8. See, for a splendid literary evocation of this type of murder, Konrad (1986), who by the way does not use the term 'witch.' Some years ago the British Anglican priest Anthony Kennedy made a splash by proposing to burn female priests as witches because they were trying to assume power that did not belong to them (cf. *Trouw d.d.* 10 March 1994).
9. But see the exceptional case of Gottliebin Dittus (Blumhardt 1972).
10. A remarkable case regarding a priest who was attacked and beaten bloody by the members of a particular sect who wanted to deliver him from the devil who allegedly took possession of him, occurred in 1926 in Bombon (France). However, the victim did not die (cf. *Nieuwe Rotterdamsche Courant Ochtend- en Avondblad* d.d. 6 January 1926).
11. See for an extensive description of this case Naegeli-Osjord (1982:155–70).
12. The expression 'ritual murder' which occurs in almost all the newspaper reports and also a few times in this paper, is interesting. The adjective 'ritual' evokes special associations, for instance, with human sacrifices as they were supposedly made by 'primitive' or 'heathen' peoples. Certain reports on the Velp case make explicit reference to 'sacrifice' (cf. *Panorama* d.d. 21–29 July 1988). It is striking that one did not represent the offenders as, for example, wild animals, but rather as 'wild,' 'uncivilized,' 'unchristian' humans. This is, I think, a consequence of the fact that when killing the baby they had indulged in a series of acts that were clearly inspired by their religious ideas. If this is not the case one often falls back on comparisons with animals devoid of reason and full of irrational impulses.
13. Besides a series of newspaper articles and a few reports in periodicals (cf. *Nieuwe Revu* d.d. 4–11 August 1988 and *Panorama* July 1988) I know of only one article that puts this case in a wider historical context in order to understand it better (see Van Belzen 1988).
14. I want to emphasize that I do not consider psychiatric diagnoses to be insignificant for gaining insight in the kind of cases presented. But I want to make clear that these diagnoses tend to be one-sided and incomplete.
15. The idea that one does something to please God comes clearly to the fore when a child dies because its parents refuse medical treatment on religious grounds. That they may be brought before court and accused of homicide, as sometimes happens, is simply inconceivable to them. On 14 October 1990 BBC 1 broadcasted a very interesting documentary on such a case in the program *Heart of the Matter*.
16. A similar case occurred among Muslims in July 1994 at Lille, where a 19-year-old girl who was said to be possessed by the Devil expired after an imam had tried to cast him out by forcing her to drink five liters of water in a short time. In the Netherlands in 1991 a man and three women were arrested because they had used rough methods to deliver two children – a son and a daughter of one of the women – from devils who had possessed them. For weeks on end the blindfolded boy was confined to a small space and 'treated' with hot irons and burning cigarettes. One of the women, a professional physician, was supposed to make sure that the regular use of physical violence did not result in the death of the victim (cf. *NRC HB* d.d. 8 June 1991). In 1994 the police of Tubbergen took three members of a religious foundation (the Padre Pio Stichting) into custody because they were suspected of having physically ill-treated a psychiatric patient during an exorcism ritual by making incisions in both her ears and by beating her black and blue (cf. *NRC HB* d.d. 7 October 1994, 11 November 1994, and 29 November 1994).
17. Due to lack of information it is sometimes difficult to distinguish an 'exorcism murder' from a 'Devil's murder.' One of them occurred, for example, in 1895 in Akersloot (the Netherlands), where a shoemaker was arrested and put into an asylum because he believed that his wife was possessed by the Devil and had therefore beaten her almost to death (cf. *Provinciale Drentsche & Asser Courant* d.d. 2 August 1895). It is impossible to find out whether exorcism was involved.
18. See for similar cases outside the Netherlands Ideler (1851:209–10) and Hellwig (1908c:378–79).
19. On each of the three cases a modest amount of literature exists. The psychiatrist Tolsma (1945) dealt with the reli-murder in the Weverwijk in his dissertation (1945). He refers to the two other cases without treating them extensively (ibid.:118–19). On the 'lugger-murders' of 1915 the physician and writer Schotman published a short story (1941) and an epic poem (1946). Van der Scheer (1917), Jelgersma (1917) and Carp (1941) refer to it. The case in Appeltern is described by Ruysch (1900) and Bouman (1901, 1906), who both were acquainted with the culprits. All other publications on this case are based on their work, for example, Jelgersma (1917), Kempe (1938), Carp (1941), Tolsma (1945), Van Rooy (1949), Zaal (1972), and Van Straten (1990). See for articles in which the three cases are analyzed in relation to each other Nagel (1960), Verrips (1987), and Van Belzen (1988). Recently Van Belzen (1996) used the case of Appeltern to show the completely different reactions to it of psychiatrists and theologians.
20. Possibly the blowpipe was not coincidental since one of the means used to cast out devils is to 'blow' the eyes and mouth of the possessed (Van Dam 1973:122).
21. For instance, an important difference is that the offenders in the case occurring in Velp were not

ultra-orthodox Calvinists but people who believed in a particular mixture of beliefs coming from both the Bible and spiritualistic literature. Another difference is that they did not believe that the coming of the Kingdom of God was near and could be speeded up by destroying Satan. In fact everything started with an effort to cast out demons who were supposed to have taken possession of one of them. Finally there are no indications that someone before or after the killing of the baby believed that he or she was the Lord or Jesus Christ. However, they claimed to have had several visions of the latter during their efforts to exorcise the baby.

22. Other important resemblances are, for example, the following: a) the fact that the offenders kept themselves busy for more than 48 hours with singing, dancing, and praying without sleeping, eating, or drinking in order to cast the demons out and b) (probably as a consequence) the appearance of all sorts of hallucinations (some of them with an undeniably sexual character).
23. A striking trait of many reli-murders is that, just as in the case of the *crime passionnel* (cf. Philips 1938), there is a close connection between the killers and the killed. Often it concerns close relatives or, if not, people who belong to close-knit groups in which the use of a kinship idiom is common. This is an intriguing phenomenon that begs for further research.
24. A case which closely resembles the one dealt with is that of father and son Alexander. They were Germans who went to the Canary Islands and in 1970 killed three members of their family in a really gruesome way because they thought them to be instruments of the Devil. Father Alexander, a member of an extreme religious society founded in the 19th century by a certain Jacob Lorber, called his son immediately after he was born a prophet of the Lord whom one had to obey in each and every respect. When the adolescent boy wanted to have sex with his mother and older sister this was therefore permitted. As his younger twin sisters talked about this with others the police developed an interest in the family, reason why father Alexander decided to emigrate to Santa Cruz on Tenerife, where he and his family lived in retirement. On 22 December 1970 father and son Alexander decided, that Mrs Alexander and her two daughters whom they perceived as 'unclean' had to be killed for the sake of a purification deemed necessary by both. And so happened. As Frank murdered his mother and two sisters and awfully maimed their bodies, his father was playing the organ and singing hymns. Especially the breasts and private parts of the victims were the direct objects of his bloody attacks. After their arrest the evildoers kept saying that they had indulged in 'a purification act' at a sacred moment in time (cf. Wilson 1988:396 ff.; Nash 1992:14/15). An equally macabre case about which I could not find much material occurred at the end of the eighties in Amsterdam. A man murdered his pregnant wife, took the baby out of her belly and killed it because he fancied that it was possessed by the Devil (cf. *Parool* d.d. 21 April 1990). Compare the case of the American Sanders, the leader of a sect, who together with a few disciples murdered a policeman in whom he had recognized the Devil in person (Wilson & Seaman 1989:294/95).
25. I think that the theory Bataille developed on the track of Hubert and Mauss with regard to transgressive acts as sacrifices could also provide some clarification here. For according to him these acts can be seen as offerings that serve to lead the sacrificers out of this world of the rational, the homogeneous, and the discontinuous into a completely different world where the earthly discontinuity does not exist and one enjoys absolute sovereignty and in a sense equals God.
26. Ger Verrips (1990:24) suggests that the reli-murder in Weverwijk, which I consider to be a clear example of a 'Devil's murder,' might be inspired by the biblical story about Abraham's sacrifice. This is unacceptable, for no data support it.
27. If one interprets the story of Abraham's sacrifice as one about the relation between God and believers independently of sex and gender, the identification becomes less striking.
28. Remarkable in the media reports is that killing one's own children and then committing suicide is often attributed to relational problems with a partner. I do not think that this is always an incorrect diagnosis, but it can easily divert attention from other possible causes, for example, the pathological elaboration of particular religious beliefs.
29. When Schubart describes and analyses religious sadism, that is, a cruel desire to devour, he does not deal with cases of reli-murder, although this would have been to the point. He talks instead about slaughtering humans who are perceived as embodiments of God and killing God himself, a kind of sacred sex killing, which is committed mainly by 'wild' people, i.c., women!
30. See for an exceptional case of self-crucifixion Ideler (1851:202 ff.).
31. See for contemporary documentation on this spectacular case *Archiv für Kriminal-Anthropologie und Kriminalistik* (1904 15:59).
32. The data on this case come from a newspaper report d.d. 29 October 1959. Unfortunately I forgot to note which newspaper published it.
33. See in this connection Bordewijk's fantastic story *In plenitudine Christi* (1981:64–68) about the members of a peasant family who became mesmerized by the assertion of a stranger that the Devil had returned to earth in the shape of their servant, and decided to crucify the poor man. This story, which is probably based on the Appeltern affair, is remarkable because it contains the ingredients of different types of reli-murders.

34. This difference is splendidly expressed in the fact that Catholics worship relics and have no trouble with the representation of the divine and holy in statues, whilst this is completely unacceptable for Protestants.
35. Illustrative examples of people who at a particular moment thought they were possessed by the Devil, while they evidently struggled with sexual problems, are those of Achille, a patient of Janet (1990), and Frank, a client of Tejirian (1990). The first suffered from remorse for adultery and the second feared his own homosexual inclinations.
36. If this view is correct, then it means that in murder cases characterized by a high degree of mutilation one has to think first of a perpetrator with a Protestant background and not a Roman Catholic one.
37. I know that my interpretation of the Müller case does not rest on a firm empirical basis. But there is often not much material available for such cases. And, if it exists, it is rather unaccessible. I would have liked, for instance, to know more about the religious background of father Alexander before he became a member of the Lorber Society. On the basis of the kind of mutilations of the bodies of his wife and two children I would dare to state that he probably was not raised as a Roman Catholic.

References

Blumhardt, C. 1978: *Die Krankheitsgeschichte der Gottliebin Dittus*. Herausgegeben und eingeleitet von Gerhard Schäfer. Mit einer Interpretation der Krankenheilung von Theodor Bovet. Göttingen.

Bordewijk, F. 1981: *Fantastische vertellingen*. 's-Gravenhage.

Bouman, L. 1901: Un cas important d'infection psychique. In: *(Actes de) Congrès international d'anthropologie criminelle (Compte Rendu des travaux de la cinquième session)* tenue à Amsterdam du 9 au 14 Septembre 1901 publié par les soins de... J.K.A. Salomonson. Amsterdam: 106 – 18.

Bouman, L. 1906: Une récidive d'infection psychique. In: *Psychiatrische en Neurologische Bladen*: 449 – 56.

Bugliosi, V. & C. Gentry 1975: *Helter Skelter. The True Story of the Manson Murders*. Toronto, New York, London.

Carp, E.A.D.E. 1941: *De psychopathieen. Inclusief de psychotische ontwikkelingsvormen op psychopathischen grondslag*. 2e herz. druk. Amsterdam.

Cohn, N. 1975: *Europe's Inner Demons. An Enquiry Inspired by the Great Witch-Hunt*. London.

De Jong, H.W.M. 1959: *Demonische ziekten in Babylon en Bijbel*. Leiden.

Frazer, J.G. 1922: *The Golden Bough. A Study In Magic and Religion*. Part I *The Magic Art and the Evolution of Kings* Vol. I. Third Edition. London.

Greenwood, S. 1995: 'Wake the Flame Inside Us.' Magic, Healing and the Enterprise Culture in Contemporary Britain. In: *Etnofoor*: 47 – 63.

Hellwig, A. 1908a: Religiöse Fanatiker. In: *Archiv für Kriminal-Anthropologie und Kriminalistik:* 186 – 87.

Hellwig, A. 1908b: *Verbrechen und Aberglaube. Skizzen aus der volkskundlichen Kriminalistik*. Leipzig.

Hellwig, A. 1908c: Ein religiöses Menschenopfer in Russland. In: *Archiv für Kriminal-Anthropologie und Kriminalistik*: 378 – 79.

Hellwig, A. 1909: Der Hexenmord zu Forchheim. In: *Der Pitaval der Gegenwart. Almanach interessanter Straffälle*: 170 – 97.

Herrmann, H. 1994: *Passion der Grausamkeit. 2000 Jahre Folter im Namen Gottes*. München.

Hubert, H. & M. Mauss [1898]: *Sacrifice: Its Nature and Function*. Transl. by W.D. Walls. London: 1964.

Ideler, K.W. 1851: *Geschiedkundige voorstellingen der verschillende vormen van godsdienstigen waanzin*. Schoonhoven.

Janet, P. 1990: *Achille. Een geval van hedendaagse duivelbezwering*. Amsterdam.

Jelgersma, G. 1917: *Leerboek der psychiatrie*. 2 Dln, 2de vermeerderde druk. Amsterdam.

Kempe, G.Th. 1938: *Criminaliteit en kerkgenootschap*. Utrecht/Nijmegen.

Konrad, G. 1986: *De medeplichtige*. Amsterdam.

La Fontaine, J.S. 1992: Concepts of Evil, Witchcraft and the Sexual Abuse of Children in Modern England. In: *Etnofoor*: 6 – 20.

Lanning, K.V. 1992: A Law-Enforcement Perspective on Allegations of Ritual Abuse. In: D.K. Sakheim & S.E. Devine (eds.), *Out of Darkness. Exploring Satanism and Ritual Abuse*. New York: 109 – 47.

Luhrmann, T.M. 1989: *Persuasions of the Witch's Craft: Ritual Magic in Contemporary England*. Harvard.

Maquart, F.X. 1948: L'exorciste devant les manifestations diaboliques. In: *Satan, Les études carmelitaines*. N.p.: 328 – 52.

Nagel, W.H. 1960: Criminality and Religion. In: *Tijdschrift voor Strafrecht*: 263 – 92.

Naegeli-Osjord, H. 1983: *Bessenheit und Exorzismus*. Remagen.

Nash, J.R. 1992: *World Encyclopedia of 20th Century Murder*. New York.

Philips, S.H. 1938: *Het passionneele misdrijf in Nederland*. Amsterdam.

Plokker, J.H. 1948: Moord uit religieuze motieven. In: E.A.D.E. Carp e.a., *Patho-psychologische bijdragen tot de kennis van het moordprobleem*. Lochem: 147 – 81.

Roper, L. 1994: *Oedipus & the Devil. Witchcraft, sexuality and religion in early modern Europe*. London.

Ruysch, 1900: Godsdienstwaanzin. In: *Psychiatrische en Neurologische Bladen*: 87 – 100.

Shapiro, M.J. 1995: Warring Bodies and Bodies Politic: Tribal versus State Societies. In: *Body & Society*: 107 – 25.

Schotman, J.W. 1941: *De blinde vaart*. Pleiaden-Reeks 6. Naarden.

Schotman, J.W. 1946: *Hellevaart*. Bayard Reeks. Bussum.

Schubart, W. 1941: *Erotiek en Religie*. Tweede druk. Haarlem.

Tejirian, E.J. 1990: *Sexuality and the devil. Symbols of love, power and fear in male psychology*. New York & London.

Tolsma, F.J. 1945: *Inductie, religieuze groepsvorming en godsdienstwaanzin. Een klinische en phaenomenologische studie*. Amsterdam.

Van Belzen, J.[A.] 1988: Moord en occultisme. In: *Intermediair* 24(51): 43 – 50.

Van Belzen, J.[A.] 1996: Godsdienst en Psychiatrie: Reacties op een geval van doodslag in godsdienstwaanzin. In: *Gewina* 19:29 – 42.

Van Dam, W.C. 1973: *Demonen Eruit, in Jezus'Naam!* Kampen.

Van Meer, R. 1988: Calvinisme of psychiatrie. Een psychiatrisch commentaar op Verrips' moorddadige interpretatie. In: *Amsterdams Sociologisch Tijdschrift*: 131 – 40.

Van Rooy, H. 1949: *Criminaliteit van stad en platteland. Nijmegen en omstreken*. Nijmegen/Utrecht.

Van Straten, H. 1990: *Moordenaarswerk. Nederlandse moordzaken die de experts verbijsterden*. Tweede herziene druk. Amsterdam.

Van der Scheer, W.M. 1917: Familiemord. Das Drama zu B. In: *Psychiatrische en Neurologische Bladen*: 194 – 211.

Verrips, G. 1990: *Vrees en vrijheid. Essays*. Amsterdam.

Verrips, J. 1987: Slachtoffers van het geloof. Drie gevallen van doodslag in Calvinistische kring. In: *Sociologisch Tijdschrift* 14: 357 – 407.

Verrips, J. 1988: Calvinisme of psychiatrie. Ge(e)n keuze. In: *Amsterdams Sociologisch Tijdschrift* 15:140 – 45.

Verrips, J. 1991: Moord en doodslag op godsdienstige gronden. Een tentatieve typologie en enige reflecties. In: *Justitiële Verkenningen* '91: 59 – 87.

Verrips, J. 1995: The State and the Empire of Evil. Paper Presented in the Panel 'Formations and Deformations: Religion and the State in Contemporary Europe' at the 94tyh Annual Meeting of the AAA at Washington, 15 – 19 November, 1995.

Wiesendanger, H. 1995: *In Teufels Küche. Jugendokkultismus: Gründe, Folgen, Hilfen*. Frankfurt am Main.

Wilson, C. 1988: *The Mammoth Book of True Crime*. London.

Wilson, C. & D. Seaman 1989: *Encyclopaedia of Modern Murder*. London.

Zaal, W. 1972: *Gods onkruid. Nederlandse sekten en messiassen*. Amsterdam.

Zeegers, G.H.L. et al. 1967: *God in Nederland. Een statistisch onderzoek naar godsdienst en kerkelijkheid in Nederland ingesteld in opdracht van De Gellustreerde Pers nv*. Amsterdam.

Producing Tradition and Managing Social Changes in the French Vineyards

The Circle of Time in Burgundy

Marion Demossier

Demossier, Marion 1997: Producing Tradition and Managing Social Changes in the French Vineyards. The Circle of Time in Burgundy. – Ethnologia Europaea 27: 47–58.

The vineyards of Burgundy have an unparalleled reputation for the quality of their wines and an image of unchanging tradition. Such clichés hide the reality of a dynamic and fluid society which has been subject to the constant pressure of social and economic change. By providing the first ethnographic study of the major regional festival, the Saint Vincent Tournante, this article demonstrates not only the methods by which local wine producers have "invented" tradition for their own commercial advantage, but also the importance of ritual to the social and professional world of the *vigneron*.

Dr Marion Demossier, School of Modern Languages and International Studies, University of Bath, Claverton Down, Bath BA2 7AY, Great-Britain. E.mail: mlsmd@bath.ac.uk

In France, tradition, origin and age are the essential contributory factors in forming the reputation of a wine. Nobody questions the quality of the ancient vineyards of Burgundy[1] and of its so-called *terroir*. The word *terroir* which is effectively untranslatable, means more in French than mere soil. It is the synonym of the land made for the culture of vines and it has also described, since at least the XVIth century, a wine or a person who has all the qualities and the defects of their place of birth. With the emergence of pedology as a science in the XIXth century, the concept of *terroir* has been presented as immanent. Man is only there to bring forth the potential[2] of this *terroir*. In France, the concept of *terroir* has been given legal expression by the *Appellation d'Origine Contrôlée* or *AOC* and its definition of the *cru*.

As they have passed from one generation to another, no real change has occurred in the geographical landscape of the renowned vineyards of Burgundy. Exploited first by the monks, later by the aristocracy and the bourgeoisie and now in the majority by families of wine growers (*vignerons*), these plots are perceived as immemorial and stable. Such permanence and continuity offer a guarantee of the quality of the vineyards and their production. Some of the most celebrated families of wine-growers have been in the same village since the XVIth century, for example the Esmonin in Gevrey-Chambertin[3] or the Barolet in Saint Romain and this is often taken to be symptomatic of a wider pattern. However, the historiography of the region and the results of my ethnological fieldwork contradicts this image of an unchanging social space. This paper[4] is the result of six months of ethnographic fieldwork in the village of Puligny-Montrachet during 1990–1991 when I participated in the organisation and management of the forthcoming festival.[5] I will argue that the Burgundian vineyards have belonged to different social groups at different stages of its history. Each succeeding class of landowners has stamped its own mark on the vineyard, most recently the families of *vignerons* who since the phylloxera crisis of 1886 have formed the predominant group of landowners. Since that crisis, different social groups have contributed to a process of "inventing tradition" which has helped them to legitimise their own status as wine growers and maintain the tradition of Burgundy's ancient wines. The aim of this article is to explore the relationship between the notion of tradition and the reality of social change in Burgundian viticulture by examining, in particular detail, a key regional festival: the Saint Vincent Tournante.

Since the publication in 1983 of the influential collection of essays edited by Eric Hobsbawm and Terence Ranger (1983) entitled "*The invention of tradition*", there has been a great deal of scholarly interest in the idea of the "invention" of the past. Robert Ulin (1986) has recently discussed some of the limits of the interpretation of the concept of tradition by scholars like Linnekin (1983) or Hanson (1989). For Robert Ulin (1995:526),

"the current status of Southwest French wines follows conjointly from their political and economic history and a process of invention that links place and individual property with the authenticity and quality of wine".

The author believes that there is much to be gained from viewing the wine growing past as invented but that not all discourses of an imagined and relativized past have an equal chance of being advanced and recognised as authoritative. In Bordeaux,

"the conjuncture of the political economy of wine-growing and the cultural representation of elite wines as authoritative has enabled elite growers to use the cultural capital associated with their wines to tremendous commercial advantage".[6]

In the example of Burgundy, I will show how the local wine-growers have taken the task of constructing tradition into their own hands. Through their increasingly powerful position in the professional sphere, they have been able to impose themselves through local associations and regional or national bodies like the *syndicat de village* or the *Bureau Interprofessionnel des vins de Bourgogne*. Their financial and numerical strength has helped them to take control of the process of construction and legitimisation of the vineyards. They have called into play the organisation and recognition of the landscape because of their economic domination of the region and the symbolic importance of their control of the whole process of wine making. By examining the festival of the Saint Vincent Tournante, it is possible to illustrate how this process works in practice.

I

The festival of the Saint Vincent Tournante takes place on the first weekend following Saint Vincent's day, the 22nd of January, in order to honour the patron saint of winegrowers. The right to host the Saint Vincent Tournante rotates amongst the winegrowing villages of the Côte de Beaune and Côte de Nuits and returns every twenty to thirty years to its point of departure. Although Saint Vincent is recognised as the patron saint of winegrowers, before the creation in 1937 of this peripatetic festival every village organised a celebration in honour of its own patron saint, who could be Saint Vincent, or another martyr such as Saint Bernard, Saint Thibeault, or Saint Cyr. Today the Saint Vincent Tournante is the established regional festival, but the cult of individual saints' days is still kept alive and is marked by a formal mass and then a banquet for the inhabitants of the village. It was these traditional celebrations that provided the model for the Saint Vincent Tournante. The village chosen for the event organises a procession attended by representatives of all of the seventy-five mutual aid societies in the region followed by a church service held in parallel with a free wine tasting, and finally the three banquets of honour.

The role of the mutual aid societies is crucial for understanding the origins of the Saint Vincent Tournante. During the Old Regime, these mutual aid societies, known as confraternities, fulfilled both a spiritual and secular function, and in times of illness or death would come to the aid of their members. Although abolished by the Revolution, they reemerged in the course of the nineteenth century and in 1865, the first modern mutual aid society was founded in Meloisey. Their role was to provide financial or physical help to the winegrowers in the event of sickness, death or other calamities. Many of these societies were closely associated with the Church. The political friction between Church and State in the period before 1914 also saw the establishment of purely secular societies. Today the winegrowers are economically independent and few require the assurance of mutual aid, but the societies continue to act as a focus of sociability and they help young winegrowers to integrate into the professional community. They also provide the structure for the organisation of the Festival of Saint Vincent Tournante.

In order to understand the festival and the local society in which it is held, it is necessary to examine the historical background of the Saint Vincent Tournante. In 1934, the *Confrérie des Chevaliers du Tastevin* was created in Burgundy (Nuits-Saint-Georges) by two local notables, Camille Rodier, the chairman of the tourist office, and Georges Faiveley, a winemerchant in Nuits-Saint-Georges. Their aim in establishing this Bacchic society was twofold. Firstly, they intended to build an attractive ritual based upon gastronomy, wine and Rabelais. Their inspiration was the statutes of a confraternity called the "Order of the drink" [7], invented by a certain Mr de la Posquières in 1703, whose activities were described later in a manuscript written by a retired colonel of the Hussards. He penned his account in 1812 and it provided the framework for a confraternity held in Beaune at that time but which disappeared soon after. The second aim of Rodier and Faiveley, but not the least important one, was the promotion of the wines of the region and more precisely those from Nuits-Saint-Georges.[8] The *Confrérie* has served as an example all over France and similar *Confréries* now promote the wines of regions such as the Loire and the Bordelais. It is also important to note that since the 1970s the *Confrérie* has issued its own special commendation for Burgundian wines called *Tastevinage*. The opportunity to participate in the competition for this label is open to all winegrowers, whose product is subject to a "blind tasting", that is to say the producer of the wine is unknown to the judges. For a wine grower to be accorded the "*Tastevinage*" label is a source of professional prestige and potentially of advantage when it comes to the commercialisation of his vintage.

The economic and social context is equally important for understanding the origins of the *Confrérie* des Chevaliers du Tastevin. The dire economic situation of the 1930s meant that demand for wine fell sharply, producing serious tensions between two very different social groups: the winegrowers and the winemerchants. It was the merchants who bought the grapes from the *vignerons*, produced and marketed the wine. When they stopped buying the grape harvest, this soon meant hardship for the winegrowers. The winemerchants themselves were also in a difficult position because they were left with large unsold and expensive stocks.

Another source of friction between winegrowers and winemerchants was the introduction of the *Appellations d'Origine Contrôlées* legislation, which involved the establishment of a hierarchical scale of quality for the different vineyards. It was not a new idea. In Bordeaux, a classification had been established in 1855 which was the first widely accepted hierarchy of wine appellations and it has changed little to the present day.[9] This classification was established in response to that requested by the organisers of the Universal Exposition of Bordeaux wines held in Paris. A similar classification was devised in Burgundy soon after by Dr Lavalle and although it initially encountered hostility, it has subsequently become the basis for the *Appellation*'s of the region's wine. The aim of this classification was to promote the wines but also to protect the production against fraud. In the context of 1930s, the *Confrérie* dominated by the local wine nobility, called the tune in the forthcoming organisation of the *Appellations*. Although, the system of *Appellations* had been tacitly recognised in 1919, it was only confirmed in 1930 with a legal decree issued by the Tribunal of Commerce of Dijon which stated that individual communes had the right to petition for an *Appellation*. This was complemented by a law of 30 July 1935 establishing the foundation of the *INAO* which declared that the individual *Appellations* were produced from a precise geographical are according to current and common practices and customs.[10]

Throughout the nineteenth and the early part of the twentieth century, the process of establishing the system of *AOC* in Burgundy was marked by two conflicting tendencies. Firstly the predominance of the large landowners who exercised a powerful influence on both a professional and institutional level. Secondly by the emergence of an increasingly powerful and vocal lobby of *vignerons* anxious to mark their own professional presence. With such sharp sources of social friction, it is clear why the *Confrérie* wanted to create a festival which would be a medium between the competing groups. Previously the large landowners had argued with the winemerchants about the limits of different appellations and had denounced the arbitrary nature of a classification based on the commercial considerations contained in the project of Dr Lavalle of 1855. Now rather surprisingly it is the *vignerons* who prepare their dossiers in favour of the right to an appellation by using, in part, the classification of Lavalle. The Saint Vincent Tournante for its part provides an additional stamp of legitimacy to recently recognised *crus* by integrating them into the ritual of the festival.

In order to alleviate the effects of the depression, several major projects were undertaken locally with the aim of promoting Burgundian wine. In 1930, Burgundy like the rest of France was experiencing a revival of interest in its folklore and tradition as is revealed by the "*Guide of the popular and traditional festival of Burgundy*" published in 1930. In its preface, the authors declared:

"Don't forget that like Provence and Brittany, you have many regional festivals, traditional and popular. Don't let them die and disappear, it is with your wine and your archaeological monuments one of the flowers of your tourism".[11]

A few years later, in 1937, the town of Beaune decided to fund the creation of a museum of wine[12] and the founding of the *Confrérie des Chevaliers du Tastevin* was another example of this trend. It was hoped that such a body would repair the relationship between the merchants and the winegrowers and give a commercial boost to Burgundian wines in the context of a grave economic crisis. It was also an attempt to encourage communication between two separate worlds: the world of the vine and the world of wine. As Fernand Woutaz declared in 1971:

"Against the difficulties of this period which seem to ruin a lot of people, don't revolt but take the Tastevin and establish the dialogue".[13]

What could better break down social barriers and remove a sense of conflict than sharing a drink?[14]

The Saint Vincent Tournante was therefore born out of the social and economic crises of the 1930s. The collapse in wine sales and the disputes about the introduction of the *AOC* legislation which was threatening to add fuel to the already combustible relations between *vignerons*, local notables and *negociants*. In this tense atmosphere, Rodier and Faiveley created the *Confrérie des Chevaliers du Tastevin*. In doing so, they drew upon the myth of an earlier Burgundian golden age of social unity, and the increasingly popular contemporary enthusiasm for local folklore and tradition. Through the costumes and pageantry of the *Chevaliers* and the Saint Vincent, they hoped to cement over social divisions and provide an economic boost to their ailing commerce. The incredible success of the enterprise would exceed even their wildest dreams.

II

Today the role of the *Confrérie* is to oversee the organisation of the festival and it is responsible for choosing the village which will hold the Saint Vincent Tournante. It is easy to see why such an administrative structure is needed. The Saint Vincent Tournante takes more than a year to prepare and the organisers need to be able to welcome as many as 100.000 visitors in two days. The budget supported by the host village and by an association created especially for this occasion is around 4.000.000 French francs. This is a fabulous sum when we consider that a village such as Puligny-Montrachet has a population of only 400 people. A number of different factors lie behind the citing of the festival. For example, when new *Appellations* were created in the Hautes Côtes de Beaune, or in Marsannay-la-Côte the Saint Vincent Tournante played a significant role in validating their enhanced status. According to M. Chevignard, responsible for the *Confrérie des Chevaliers du Tastevin*:

"When there is a new *Appellation*, we study the question with the winegrowers and if they agree, we use Saint Vincent".[15]

But the *Confrérie* also reinforces the position of the more famous villages by allowing them to hold the festival every twenty or thirty years.

The *Confrérie* helps to maintain the ethic and the original sense of what is now an enormous festival by supervising the preparations and by suggesting alterations where necessary. For example, during the meetings to prepare the Saint Vincent Tournante of Puligny-Montrachet, the wine-growers suggested opening the cellars and offering wine tastings at 9 a.m., well before the church service and mass. The reaction was a very clear and quick no from the *Confrérie* because they wanted to maintain the religious side of this popular event. This is a very good example of their role, it also reveals the different political and ideological values of the social groups involved. The festival highlights conflicting religious values, those of the wine notability, on the one hand, and that of the winegrowers on the other, and it is possible to detect traditional political divisions between clericalism and anti-clericalism. Puligny-Montrachet we should note had possessed two mutual aid societies, one catholic the other secular until 1914, and in the neighbouring village of Pommard the division between the lay *Union of the wine-growers* and the Catholic *Society of Saint Vincent* still exists today. On the whole, however, it is fair to say that relations with the church are now harmonious. The sermons of local priests stress the fundamental role of wine in Christian ritual, immortalised in the words of chanoine Kir, clergyman and mayor of Dijon, who in 1937 spoke of "Le vin de l'éloquence sacrée".

The *Confrérie*, through the Saint Vincent Tournante and its other activities, tries to play the role of a medium between two connected but hostile worlds: the winegrowers who are the most numerous and powerful in the village and the handful of large landowners or winemerchants. The latter traditionally formed the social elite, or bourgeoisie, of the region; they owned the largest and most prestigious plots but never worked directly in the vines. In the past, the village was marked by these social divisions and it is still vital to understanding the contemporary social organisation. In the daily discourses and practices, the winegrowers define themselves as "workers in the vineyard"[16] and describe the landlords as those who "don't work in the vineyard".[17] Their respective habits, clothes, hands, gesture and language illustrate two separate social worlds. The attempts of the *Confrérie* to build bridges between these two social groups can be seen in their invitation of two representatives of each of the seventy-five mutual aid societies to their banquet.

In fact, the banquets themselves provide eloquent testimony to the social, professional and cultural world of the vineyards. At midday on the Saturday of the Saint Vincent Tournante, three banquets are held in different parts of the region. One is the banquet of the local priests organised in the host village by a catholic landlord, the second is the banquet of the winegrowers and their guests (customers, foreign and French winemerchants…); and the last one is the banquet of the Clos-de-Vougeot organised by the *Confrérie* in its fief, the chateau of Clos-Vougeot, and it is remarkable for its prestigious public of international celebrities, politicians and businessmen. Through this tripartite division, we can glimpse the three medieval orders: Church, Nobility and Third Estate which was almost certainly the original intention of its authors in 1937.

Another important function of the *Confrérie* is the *Intronisation* of new members.[18] Every year, the village which hosts the festival proposes a list of the oldest and most worthy winegrowers from the village. These winegrowers are received into the *Confrérie des Chevaliers du Tastevin* following the ritual incantation of "Noé, Bacchus, Saint Vincent". This quasi-religious rite offers a public recognition of their career as worker of the vineyard. It is a consecration of their position in the community and the village. As one *vigneron* declared of his father: "To be received with the oldest winegrowers of the village, it was something for him".[19]

This part of the festival is a key point for our understanding of the local community in terms of family lineage, identities, social capital and belonging. The village is composed of different families of winegrowers some of whom have lived there since the XVIth century. Traditionally, the winegrowers were tied to their ancestors not only through their work in the vines, but also to the wine itself via the foundation of perpetual masses for their ancestors paid for by wine from their annual production.[20] Every generation brings something new to the lineage by adding agricultural, technical or commercial skills, or land to the family patrimony. It is the family name of the vigneron that is conspicuous in the Burgundian wine industry. Unlike wine elsewhere in France, it is the vigneron's name on the bottle that is the most important element, not just the particular parcel of vines or, as in Bordeaux, the Château.

The role of the mutual aid society in the festival is to control the success of the Saint Vincent Tournante in terms of gaining economic, social and symbolic weight and assuring a balance in the budget. It is also a method of creating tradition. The festival is in the hands of the principal members of the mutual aid society. These winegrowers who are in many cases the most important economic and social individuals in the village take the key decisions. One big change help to explain how the event is perceived and directed by the producers. The money invested in the Saint Vincent Tournante has been increasing steadily since the 1950s, and between 1959 and 1988, it has multiplied thirtyfive times. In 1961, two hundred people came to Puligny-Montrachet, but by 1991 more than 100.000 visited the village during the weekend of 20–22 January. From a small and traditional event, it has been transformed into a major commercial and public venture using all the techniques of the modern media. The organisation in 1991 was handled by ten committees and the festival was covered by the local, national and international press. The mass was broadcast live in the village. Yet the underlying aim of this gargantuan festival remains the confirmation of the legitimacy of the village's vineyards and the quality of their wines. The question is how can a local festival create tradition and reputation, or help to manage the effects of social change. Are the images, discourses and identities produced by the local people really effective in the broader context of the world winemarket?

III

In order to answer these questions, we have to analyse more precisely how the Saint Vincent Tournante and its organisation fulfils an important function in the construction of a local and even national identity. Wine is crucial to the social exchanges within the professional community of winegrowers and this is central to the festival. Every year, the host village proposes a free winetasting organised by the winegrowers and landlords of the village. In Puligny-Montrachet, three vintages were prepared for this purpose: one of wine harvested in 1982 consisting of 4.000 bottles, another from the grapes of 1986 of 6.000 bottles and finally that of 1988 totalling 20.000 bottles. The economic value of the gift is considerable. The grapes used in the production of these wines were collected from the individual wine producers in the village and the wine made by the elites of the local society, one landlord and three important winegrowers. The preparation of these vintages takes different forms from one village to another. Sometimes, the vintage comes from a declared stock; but sometimes it appears as if by magic, that is to say it is undeclared for tax purposes. The local authorities have long turned a blind eye to this practice, although since 1992 the tax office has been showing an increasing interest. Their concern is perhaps linked to the fact that every year, the size of this "free production" has been growing, revealing competition between villages.

Another way of seeing this competition is by examining the structure of landownership in the local vineyards. The winegrowers of Puligny-Montrachet own vines in their own village, but they also have plots in the surrounding villages. Certain of these villages are in what can be described as "compatibility of production" with Puligny-Montrachet. For instance, Meursault and Puligny-Montrachet both produce Chardonnay and prestigious *Appellations* and they are therefore in competition. Puligny-Montrachet and Pommard are, on the other hand, complementary to each other. They produce different sorts of wines, quality white and red wines respectively, and are thus compatible in terms of production. A winegrower is happy to have both of them to sell in his cellar. Moreover, the *vigneron* plays with this variety in order to improve his image. This notion of "compatibility of production" is also essential for understanding the social tactic of buying lands and the adaptive character of the domain. It is defined by social affinities such as traditional exchanges or professional solidarity, or by cultural ties, for example, the organisation of festivals or masses. Technical factors can also play a part, notably the vinification of the same variety of vine usually pinot noir or chardonnay. There is a strong resemblance between some villages in terms of the nature and quality of their wines. The festival in switching from a village of the *Côte de Beaune* to one of the *Côte de Nuits*, from a vineyard of red to white reflects this hierarchy and the compatibility of production. We could therefore say that the festival of Saint Vincent works to the advantage of all by promoting the value of Burgundy's wines.

The professional hierarchy between villages is different from the commercial one established by the wine-merchants. Overall, there are different classifications and different customers. It is something which is constantly changing and is illustrated by the gift of wine during the festival. The position of a new *Appellation* within the broader winecommunity is, in part, determined through the Festival. The gift, as Marcel Mauss has shown, obliges the person receiving it to reciprocate. This obligation takes place in the peripatetic festival and has been transformed into a massive and collective gift. The festival is turning and the gift also. This enormous circle of gifts creates an obligation and a competition for all the members of the professional community. This circularity is also a ritual which offers protection against an adverse economic situation. It is true that the offering of gifts obliges the winegrowers to compare their production with that of others. By the same token, the economic value of the gift is used for an evaluation within the professional community and is related to the position of the village in the winehierarchy. Two factors are available to judge its value: the number of bottles and the different year of the wine. For example, Puligny-Montrachet is considered to be a very prestigious village, owning some of the most famous wines in France. Its choice was, therefore, to offer 30.000 bottles of wine from three different vintages 1982, 1986, 1988 more than the neighbouring Hautes-Côtes which organised the festival the year before. The more vintages offered, the greater the value of the gift. Every one of them assesses its position and gives in relation to its position in the market. When a new *Appellation* has been granted, the successful village has to demonstrate to the rest of the community its enhanced position. The Festival of Saint Vincent Tournante is one way to be evaluated and accepted by others.

By buying a glass at 25 French francs, the visitors are able to taste the wines for free. However, the gift won't be the same for everybody. Access to different wines is determined by social and professional status. For the visitors coming mainly from the nearest departments, it is the youngest year which is proposed in the cellars. The representatives of the mutual aid societies on the other hand, have the right to taste the oldest vintage during their *casse-croûte* before the procession. The *Confrérie des Chevaliers du Tastevin* also has the privilege of sharing this wine even if they only follow part of the procession. This control of access to the winetasting reflects different values both inside and outside the community. At the same time, during all the preparation of the festival, the gift and the circulation of wines will be encouraged. The local institutions and certain national bodies like the *Office National des Forêts*, the Police and the *EDF-GDF* are all thanked for their contribution by the gift of wines. By the gift and the countergift, everybody is evaluated and evaluates the other. The aim is to secure their position in the region's

Fig. 1. The procession of the mutual aid societies of Burgundy in Puligny-Montrachet.

winehierarchy. At different times in the course of the weekend the public participating in the festival changes. The banquet of the winegrowers, given over to the celebration of the local wines, provides one example. Gastronomy adds its own prestige to the festival and to the village, and the wines are chosen in harmony with the finest delicacies. The grand *cru* Bâtard-Montrachet will be associated only with a lobster which will enhance the value of the local wine.

The procession of the mutual aid societies also plays an important part in this process of definition. The participants with their banners and effigies of the saints follow the old route of the famous *crus*, therefore all the community, winegrowers and landlords can visualise the name of the plots, their position and worth, and who owns them. The vineyard is divided into small plots with, in the case of the landlords and notables, their name on the wall of the field. This social structure is easily legible from the landscape. As Mr Carillon described the procession of Puligny-Montrachet:

"It will going down the hill to begin with, then it will pass between the Clavoillon and the Folatières, above the Pucelles and it will going down again in the direction of the grands *crus*, the road of Chassagne, near the Bâtard-Montrachet".[21]

After seeing these geographical landmarks, it is easier when tasting the wines to remember the plot. It helps to legitimise the concept of *terroir*.

The winetasting takes place in the morning and is defined by different forms of sociability. For the Burgundians and even for the guests of the winemerchants, it is a privilege to taste wine from the area without having to pay a lot of money. In fact, because the festival is in the hands of a social group, the winegrowers, who until very recently were peasants, there is a prodigious democratisation of the consumption of wine. The idea is to keep the winetasting as a form of gift, although it has some inconveniences. By Saturday afternoon the Festival has been transformed into a popular and alcoholic event. It is above all the young people who

Fig. 2. The social structure of the vineyard and the geographical landmarks of the landlords.

finish completely drunk and in 1991 no less than 40 were treated for the state of alcoholic coma. It is hardly surprising that they are accused of ruining the image of the Festival. This process shows the popular origins of the *vignerons* who want to keep their wine affordable despite the luxury character of their product. From this discussion, it is clear that for the village hosting the festival the aim is to accumulate prestige and respect for its wines from both the professional community and the outside world.

On one level, therefore, the festival is an enormous advertising campaign for the host village with its wines offered to thousands of visitors in a display of pride and publicity. More importantly, it offers an opportunity for the villages to situate themselves within the professional hierarchy. Those who have recently acquired the status of an *Appellation* can justify their enhanced position through the festival, while a long-established and internationally renowned village such as Puligny-Montrachet has an opportunity to confirm its status. Yet the festival also provides a mirror in which the participants have a chance to glimpse their own place in the social and professional sphere.

IV

The village plays a key-function in the social construction of tradition. It represents the locality in a changing world. It is associated clearly with the *crus* and most of the time, the *crus* have given their name to the village. For example, Montrachet to Puligny, Chambertin to Gevrey, Corton to Aloxe. It is helpful to consider this association of the village and its wines and how it relates to the of Saint Vincent Tournante. In 1991, the village of Puligny-Montrachet was composed of two winemerchants, one landlord, around 10 big winegrowers, some small *vignerons* (22 have between 1 and 5 hectares) and finally some parttime workers.[22] It is the landlord and the group of wealthy owners who were primarily responsible for organising the event. Although the social structure has been largely static since 1930, with a small number of notables and the large majority of *vignerons*, there is nevertheless an ongoing process of renewal.[23]

By emphasising the importance of the *terroir* and also of the wines and their owners or producers, reputation and tradition are constructed while helping to disguise the reality of social change. The collective memory incorporates the recent transformations and presents them as part of a seamless fabric that helps the society to preserve and guarantee its social ties and its hierarchy. The vineyards are central to this process and they provide a social cement for a changing community. But time is essential for the complete integration of a new family into the community. The collective memory has not forgotten the old social structure and it was expressed on many occasions during the festival by the most important landlord of the village: "To be part of the village, you need three graves in the cemetery or fifty years of being part of the community".[24]

Belonging to the village is determined by this cultural pattern. Like the vineyard with a new Appellation which needs two festivals in order to acquire legitimacy, the workers of the vines need fifty years, or two Saint Vincent Tournante, to be completely accepted as part of the community.

We must also remember that family lineage, defined in patriarchal terms, is essential to this culture. The recognition of the lineage in the social structure not only passes through the family and its reputation in the social space of the village but also through the professional community which confers its own legitimacy. In the village, the individual is defined above all in terms of his family, whose name adorns not only the houses and property, but also the plots in the vineyards where the name of their owners is frequently displayed, helping to reinforce the association between the prestige of the *crus* and that of the family. The local society registered slowly all these transformations. In everyday conversation, the population continues to maintain categories like Landlord/Winegrower which are related to the evolution of this society. They also remember the notability associated to the big properties. As one *vigneron* said of a former mayor:

"Chartron, he was elected two times, he was a winemerchant and landlord. At the time, we appreciated having a mayor with an important social situation. He shielded us with his body".[25]

Despite the appearance of an unchanging social landscape provided by the continuing importance of notable families, there is nevertheless a process of social change which the Saint Vincent Tournante facilitates. As a new inhabitant of Puligny explained matters: "Me, I took part in the Saint Vincent because I needed recognition".[26]

Whether they have lived in the village for centuries or are new to the community, the families share the stresses and strains arising from the preparation of the Saint Vincent Tournante. The organisation of the festival creates a tension between the different participants because the host village is not guaranteed to recoup its investment. The only way to make money is to sell glasses and to welcome a great number of visitors. The financial risk is enormous and millions of francs could be lost if there was an inopportune blizzard or other calamity. With this sword of Damocles suspended above them, the relationships between the organisers are very intense in the days preceding the festival. Yet this is more than compensated for by the sense of solidarity that unites the villagers as they work together for this communal expression of professional pride. The degree of financial brinkmanship has also to some extent been mitigated by the fact that the Saint Vincent Tournante, as a rotating festival, has bred a sense of solidarity and mutual obligation between the participating villages. In the event of a deficit, the money collected on earlier occasions will be used to help the losing commune. When the village makes a profit, it has to decide how to spend it. Usually, the community invests in roads, the promotion of its wines, and its tourism or the restoration and improvement of the village. In 1991, after more than 12 months of hard work, worry and preparation, the villagers of Puligny-Montrachet realised 800.000 French francs of profit.

V

The Saint Vincent Tournante is a symbol of both tradition and modernity, of old structures and the new power of the winemakers, of individualism and solidarity. The festival gives the impression of stability, creating a collective memory and provoking the recollection of past time. From this, it would seem that the Saint Vincent Tournante has served as a way of facilitating and even legitimising social change. Returning regularly to each village, it allows the inhabitants to praise the qualities of their wines to local, national and even international visitors, reinforcing the impression of unchanging tradition while frequently integrating new wine makers or *Appellations* as part of the apparently seamless tapestry of Burgundian viticulture. The contradictions between the 'gift' of wine and need to make a profit, or of the conflicts between landlords and *negociants* on one hand, and winegrower on the other shows how it is crucial for this rural society to maintain its stability in a modern changing world of competition. The only way to distinguish Burgundy from the other wines of the world is to propose its unique geography, time and proofs[27] as regional and even national emblems. Tradition creates value and offers a point of comparison to measure the evolution of the local society and its wines over time. Through this newly invented tradition of the Saint Vincent Tournante, it is possible to demonstrate how a new group of wine-makers has to a large extend taken control of wine production. They have achieved an equilibrium with the landlords and *negociants* developing a mutually rewarding partnership which maintains their respective identities through the rituals of Saint Vincent and the *Chevaliers du Tastevin*. By inventing tradition and by reconstructing their past, they define themselves and help to structure the identity of Burgundian viticulture in a competitive and changing world. This identity distinguishes Burgundy from other vineyards by a manipulation of tradition based on the concepts of notoriety, origin and age or by ... the Circle of Time.

Notes

1. There are four different appellations : regional (38% of the Burgundian surface), villages (37%), premiers crus (20%) and grands crus. Three quarters of the surface is planted in Pinot noir. Overall, there are 1.400 exploitations in Burgundy.
2. See Bérard, Laurence & Marchenay, Philippe. 1995: Lieux, temps et preuves, la construction sociale des produits de terroir. In: *Terrain,* 24, mars : 159.
3. I would like to thank Dr Mack Holt for providing me with this information.
4. I would like to thank the Ministry of the Culture in France, The Mission du Patrimoine ethnologique, the Direction Régionale des Affaires Culturelles in Burgundy and the Museum of Wine in Beaune for their grant which made this research possible.
5. This research contributed to a wider study of the cult of saints amongst winegrowers in Burgundy and formed part of my doctoral thesis on the transmission of knowledge and technical practices in the Burgundian vineyards. See Demossier, Marion 1995: *Le cru, la cuvée, le vigneron et le village: une anthropologie des communautés viti-vinicoles en Bourgogne.* Thèse de Doctorat en Anthropologie sociale, Ecole des Hautes Etudes en Sciences Sociales. To be published in 1997.
6. Ulin, Robert. C. 1995:526.
7. "L'Ordre de la Boisson".
8. There is still competition between the two côtes and the towns of Beaune and Nuits-Saint-Georges. The influence of the Dioceses shown by Roger Dion and the organisation of the market explained the bipartition of this area.
9. Ulin, Robert. 1995:22.
10. It means simply tradition.
11. "Bourguignons,
    N'oubliez pas qu'à l'instar de la Provence et de la Bretagne, vous possédez un splendide faisceau de fêtes régionalistes, traditionnelles et populaires. Ne les laissez pas mourir et disparaître, c'est, avec votre vin et vos monuments archéologiques l'un des plus beaux fleurons de votre couronne touristique".
    Association pour le renaissance des fêtes populaires bourguignonnes (1930:1).
12. Demossier, Marion & Jacobi, Daniel 1994: La bouteille de Bourgogne, entre recherche et esthétique. In: *La Revue,* Musée des Arts et Métiers, juin, 24–30.
13. "Contre les difficultés du moment qui semblaient mettre en cause les moyens traditionnels d'existence de milliers d'honnêtes gens, mieux valait lever non pas l'étendard de la révolte mais le pacifique Tastevin et instaurer le dialogue". Woutaz, Fernand (1971:65).
14. An important contribution on the Anthropology of Drink has been made by Mary Douglas (1987).
15. "Quand il y a une nouvelle appellation, on étudie

la question avec les intéressés et s'ils le souhaitent, on met Saint Vincent à leur service".
Mr. Chevignard.
16. "travailleurs de la vigne".
17. "ne vont pas à la vigne".
18. "Intronisations". The Confrérie was one of the first to create and to use this ritual.
19. "Etre intronisé avec les vieux vignerons du village, c'est quelque chose pour lui".
20. I would like to thank again Dr Mack Holt for this comment.
21. "Il va descendre de la montagne pour le départ, on passe dans les grands crus entre les Clavoillon et les Folatières, au dessus des Pucelles et ça va descendre vers les grands crus, la route de Chassagne, vers les Bâtard-Montrachet".
Mr. Carillon.
22. The social composition of Puligny is mainly people working in the neighbouring towns like Beaune or Chagny and part time workers in the wine industry.
23. The vignerons were a social group that was relatively affluent before the phylloxera crisis of 1880.
24. "Pour être du village, il faut trois tombes au cimetière ou cinquante ans d'existence au village".
Mr. Leflaive.
25. "Chartron, il a dû faire deux mandats, il était négociant en vins, propriétaire, à l'époque, on aimait avoir un maire avec une situation sociale importante, il servait de bouclier".
M. Virot.
26. "Moi, j'ai pris ça parce qu'on avait besoin de se faire reconnaître". Mr.Vallot.
27. Bérard, Laurence & Marchenay, Philippe. 1995: Lieux, temps et preuves, la construction sociale des produits de terroir. In: *Terrain*, 24, mars: 153–164.

References

Association pour la Renaissance des Fêtes Populaires Bourguignonnes. 1930: *Guide des Fêtes populaires et traditionnelles de la Bourgogne.* Mâcon, Combier.

Bérard, Laurence, & Marchenay, Philippe 1995: Lieux, temps et preuves, la construction sociale des produits de terroir. In: *Terrain,* 24, mars : 153–164.

Demossier, Marion 1995: *Le cru, la cuvée, le vigneron et le village : la transmission des pratiques et savoir-faire en Côte bourguignonne.* Paris, Thèse de Doctorat en Anthropologie sociale, Ecole des Hautes Etudes en Sciences Sociales. To be published in 1997 by the Editions Universitaires de Dijon.

Dion, Roger 1959 (1980): *Histoire de la vigne et du vin en France.* Servin, réedition Flammarion.

Douglas, Mary 1987: *Constructive Drinking, Perspectives on Drink from Anthropology.* Cambridge University Press, Maison des Sciences de l'Homme.

Grivot, Françoise 1964: *Le commerce des vins de Bourgogne.* Paris, Editions Sabri.

Hanson, Allan 1989: The Making of the Maori: Culture Invention and Its Logic. In: *American Anthropologist,* 91 (4):890–902.

Hobsbawm, Eric & Ranger, Terence 1983: *The invention of tradition.* Cambridge University Press.

Linnekin, Jocelyn 1983: Defining Tradition: Variations on the Hawaiian identity. In: *American Ethnologist,* 10: 241–252.

Loftus, Simon 1993: *Journal of a village in Burgundy.* London.

Ulin, Robert. C. 1986: Social Change through a Southwest French Wine Cooperative. In: *Ethnologia Europaea. Journal of European Ethnology* (16), 1:25–38.

Ulin, Robert C. 1988: Cooperation or cooptation: A southwest French Wine Cooperative. In: *Dialectical Anthropology,* 13 (3):253–267.

Ulin, Robert C. 1995: Invention and Representation as Cultural Capital, Southwest French Winegrowing History. In: *American Anthropologist,* 97 (3): 526.

Woutaz, Fernand 1971: *Le grand livre des Confréries des vins de France.* Paris, Editions Halevy.

Next Year in Jerusalem

A Symbolic Study of a Jewish Ritual

Daniel Meijers

Meijers, Daniel 1997: Next Year in Jerusalem. A Symbolic Study of a Jewish Ritual. – Ethnologia Europaea 27: 59–66.

During the festival of *Pesach* Jews all over the world celebrate the Exodus of the Jewish people out of Egyptian bondage with a nighttime ritual. As a result of the isolated position in which Jews have found themselves in the diaspora historically, this ritual, in which fundamental values such as exile, redemption and Jewish homeland are symbolically expressed, remained almost unchanged over the years. In fact, recently, its significance has increased as a result of the political circumstances in the Middle East. To understand Jewish feelings about this subject, it is important to realize that the same fundamental values are at stake here.

Professor Daniel Meijers, Vrije Universiteit of Amsterdam, Faculty of Socio-Cultural Studies, De Boelelaan 1081c, NL-1081 HV Amsterdam, The Netherlands.

Introduction[1]

The festival of *Pesach* or Passover, as it is called in the English-speaking world, is widely recognized as holding a primary place in the Jewish religious calender. Jew and non-Jew alike are aware of the key function the festival, especially the evening meal called the *Seder*, possesses in Jewish ritual observance[2]. The fact that the importance of *Pesach* is taken for granted even by many secular, non-observant Jews is all the more reason to attempt to investigate the nature of the festival.[3]

Held in Israel on the first night only and elsewhere on both the first and second nights of *Pesach*, the *Seder* concludes with a short prayer full of hope "Next Year in Jerusalem" which can be seen as the ultimate message of *Pesach*. Now, as a result of the events in the Middle East this festival has been re-imbued with political and religious symbols.

Although the *Seder* ritual has not remained precisely the same throughout its long history, the basic ritual, handed down from generation to generation, is, in essence unchanged. A further aspect to examine, then, is the reason for the continued existence of the *Seder* in Judaism.

In this paper, I will analyze the various stages and aspects of the *Seder*. In particular I will explore the changing emphasis over the last half century that some parts of the ritual have received among European Jews. Further, I will illustrate that this ritual contains a multitude of symbolic meanings which have always been essential to Judaism in the past and have not lost their relevance today. At the same time, I will show which social conditions have contributed to the long survival of the *Seder* observance.

The Seder Observance

The general meaning of the Hebrew word *Seder* is 'order'. In this case, *Seder* means the particular, step-by-step order which this ritual meal follows. Taking place, as it does, at the beginning of the *Pesach* festival, the *Seder* meal is held at home in the company of family and friends. Among European Jews the *Seder* always took an important place in the religious calendar. Even during the Second World War, Jews tried to observe the *Seder* ritual.

In 1943, in the Dutch concentration camp Westerbork a few families gathered around the table to hold a *Seder*. The man who led the *Seder* was trying to come to terms with the loss of a child. Another child had undergone an operation in extremely primitive circumstances. The leader of the *Seder* began to read from the traditional text. A woman who sat alone on a three-tiered bunk-bed asked if she could take part. The leader answered her from the text: "All who are hungry may come and eat, and all who are in need may come and celebrate the festival of *Pesach* together with us" (my translation from Haggadah shel Pesach).[4]

The *Seder* with its message of hope and comfort was even observed in the most difficult circumstances as a ritual emphasizing *communitas* in the sense Turner gave to this concept, i.e. a moment of anti-structure, in which feelings of human equality resist the pressure of the established hierarchical order (cf. Turner 1969:96 ff.).

The actual observance of the *Seder* is as follows: On the first night of *Pesach* the *Haggadah* is read. The text relates the miraculous Exodus of the Jewish people from slavery in Egypt. Depending on the level of religious knowledge of the participants, various explanations of the Haggadah are offered since "the more one relates (about the Exodus – D.M.) the more one is to be praised" (Haggadah shel Pesach). Certain ritually prescribed foods and dishes are then eaten and four cups of wine are drunk in the course of the meal.

The *Seder* begins with a verbal consecration

of the festival, after which the first cup of wine is drunk. The four cups of wine are linked to the four expressions of redemption employed in the Pentateuch in connection with the liberation of the Jewish people from Egypt. Then the youngest of those present asks four questions. The rest of the *Haggadah* can be considered a response to these four questions.

On the *Seder* table is a special plate with three *matzot* (unleavened bread), on the top left-hand side is an egg, on the top right a bone, in the centre the bitter herbs – usually a piece of horseradish. Below on the left is a piece of vegetable: an onion, a potato or radish, and below on the right is a dish consisting of a mixture of apple, almonds, wine and, depending on local custom, various other ingredients. Finally, below in the middle there is a quantity of bitter vegetables, mostly a bitter-tasting lettuce. The *matzah* symbolizes the speed with which the Jewish people had to leave Egypt once the time of their deliverance had arrived. There was not even time for the bread to rise: the clear implication here, is that the future Messianic redemption will also occur in the twinkling of an eye. The unleavened bread also symbolizes a more personal aspect of redemption. Ordinary leavened bread is "risen" – this refers to the "fermenting" process within the person. The ideal person does not possess the egotism and arrogance of the leavened person. He reduces himself to the level of the flat unleavened bread. *Matzah* is also, therefore, the bread of affliction, the bread of poverty, of insignificance. The three *matzot* together symbolize the unity of the Jewish people, consisting as it does of three ritual categories, priests, Levites and ordinary Jews. The egg is a reminder of the offerings brought in the Temple in connection with the festival. It is also a reminder of death, since eggs are eaten as part of the mourning ritual following the loss of a close relative. The bone is a reminder of the Paschal lamb offering. The Paschal lamb is also a symbol of survival, since in the last moments before the Exodus, the Jews had to smear the blood of a lamb on their doorposts in order that their houses should be recognized as Jewish homes. In this way, they would be "passed-over" during the tenth plague, the death of the firstborn. The various kinds of bitter herbs – horseradish, lettuce and so on, are a symbol of the bitter times of slavery. The Hebrew word for bitter vegetables is *maror*. The mixture of apple and wine comes as a contrast to the bitter herbs. It is also reminiscent of the cement which the Jews used in Egypt to make bricks.

There is yet another aspect of the contrast between life and death which exists in the *Seder*. The bitter herbs refer to the bitter persecution in Egypt when Pharaoh, the king of Egypt, decreed that all male babies were to be drowned in the Nile. On the other hand, the apples in the sweet cement-like mixture are a symbol of life: the women gave birth to their children under the apple trees, so that the Egyptians would not realize that a Jewish child had been born.[5]

Finally, the reason why the vegetable on the *Seder* plate is dipped in salt water at the commencement of the *Seder* is in order to awaken the curiosity of any children who may be present.

Of course, many other comments could be made on the *Seder*. It is, however, not my intention to give a detailed analysis and explanation of every aspect of the *Seder*. This is not only because Gruber Fredman (1983) has already done a deep study of the *Seder* but also because I wish to delineate in its "totality" the specific message which is today being propagated by this ritual. It may even be possible that aspects of the *Seder* which previously received little emphasis, are now coming more sharply into focus.

For this reason, it is important to establish that the *Seder* is connected with 'liberation' or 'redemption'. This is already apparent at the beginning. The *Seder* begins with the drinking of the first of the four cups of wine. Wine is a symbol of freedom. This can be seen from the fact that a fifth cup is also filled, by some at the beginning of the *Seder* and by others at a later stage of the ritual. There is a difference of opinion among the sages of the *Talmud* as to whether there are four, or five, expressions of 'redemption' in the Torah and consequently as to whether four or five cups of wine must be drunk at the *Seder*. As a result of this difference of opinion, a fifth cup of wine is filled, but not drunk, in expectation of the appearance of the prophet Elijah. Before the coming of the Messiah, Elijah will solve all disagreements and differences of opinion. Moreover, he is the prophet who will announce the anticipated Messianic redemption of the future. Then after the first cup of wine is drunk, the ritual recital of the story of the Exodus begins with the asking of the Four Questions "Why is this night different from all other nights?". The answer begins: "We were slaves in Egypt" and the liturgical recital of the *Haggadah* concludes with the words "Next year in Jerusalem".

I hope to show that in the course of the *Seder* a number of values and ideas emerge which are fundamental to Judaism both on an individual level and a collective level. As Gruber Fredman notes:

"The story of the Exodus contains within it a rationale for the existance of the Jews as an eternally distinct people, and also provides a metaphor for the Jews' existence as a socially marginal community. (...) Exodus deals with matters of separation and distinction, but Exodus is also a story of passages, of transitional states between fixed points, between absolute slavery in Egypt and absolute freedom in the Promised Land. (...) Exodus is the story that once and for all times has given Jews their self-definition as a people (...)" (1983:24).

It may be clear that, particularly in extreme circumstances, the *Seder* functioned as a ritual passage from slavery to freedom. Not only during the Second World War but also in Eastern Europe under communist rule *Pesach* was celebrated as 'our holiday of liberty' (Gilbert 1985:196). It is necessary to analyze this ritual in more detail to understand its meaning as a ritual of identification of the individual with a collective identity.

The Pesach Haggadah

An extremely interesting aspect of the *Haggadah* is that it is composed on a question and answer basis. This interrogatory character always exists. If, for example, no child is present to ask the four questions, they are recited by one of the adults. If a person conducts the *Seder* alone, then he recites the four questions on his own. Of all the explanations for the various customs of the *Seder* offered by the sages the most prevalent is that any children present should be stimulated to ask questions.

The *Seder*, then, can be construed as a ritual involving question and answer. Symbolically, to ask a question is to emphasize that something is unknown. By giving answers to the question, the unknown becomes known. Obviously, the questioner must be one who does not yet know the answer. Such a one is the youngest member of the group, preferably a child. A child is still unacquainted with life and the purpose of life. The answer is given by the leader of the ritual, the one who does know. In other words, asking questions indicates concealment and giving answers revelation. Thus, the significance of the *Seder* might be that, through the posing of questions, what was concealed becomes revealed.

The existence of such an important and recurring traditional ritual as the *Seder* should also lead us to investigate whether any other cultural categories receive special emphasis. This is certainly the case with day and night, as can be seen immediately at the beginning of the *Seder*. The four questions begin with relatively general questions "Why is this night different from all other nights?" Moreover, the *Seder* takes place at nightfall which is also the beginning of the Jewish day. The reason is "It was evening, it was morning, the first day" (Genesis 1:5). Based on this text, the evening is considered to be the start of a new day.

In the concealment of darkness the revealed light of the dawn lies hidden. This theme is made explicit in the *Haggadah* with the story which is related about the sages who met together to celebrate the *Seder*. They were so involved in telling the story of the Exodus from Egypt, that they did not notice that dawn had already broken. Their students came to inform that it was time to recite the morning prayer.

One of the leading Jewish scholars, the late Rabbi M.M. Schneerson, the so-called Rabbi of Lubavitch, gives the following explanation of this incident: the sages referred to in the *Haggadah* were numbered amongst the great teachers of Judaism. Their students stood on a lower spiritual level. The "light" radiated by the teachers had the effect of illuminating the souls of the students to such an extent that they thought that the dawn i.e. the Messianic redemption, had broken. The teachers, who possessed souls which were "higher" than their students, needed more illumination to attain redemption than their students, whose "lower" souls were able to find fulfilment at an earlier level through the corrective actions of their teachers (Schneerson 1962:539–540). The theme of concealment and revelation is evident in both aspects of the story that of the pupils and their teachers and that of the night becoming day.

The symbolic importance of night is also evident in the *Talmud*. This comprehensive work, treats all religious duties and practices as well as a number of cosmological ideas. The *Talmud* begins with the question of when the evening prayer should be recited. The answer is "From the time that the priests may begin to eat their 'heave-offering'" (Talmud Brachot 2A). The time indicated here is the time when stars appear in the sky. It is only at a later stage that the question of when the morning prayer may be recited is discussed. The sages of the *Talmud* continue by discussing why the evening prayer is mentioned before the morning prayer. The answer given is that in the Biblical account of the Creation, the evening of each day is mentioned before the morning.

The fact that Judaism's most outstanding religious work which was composed in the first centuries of the Diaspora commences with the theme of night followed by day, signifies that its main focus is on exile and redemption. The presentation of this theme in a question and answer framework is an indication that the Messianic redemption from exile – the morning – is viewed as a revelation which emerges from the darkness of the night. Nightfall is not defined here as when the stars first appear in the sky – the usually Talmudic definition of night – but as equivalent to the time when priests, having been ritually purified following a period of ritual impurity, may once again eat of the offering of grain which they receive as their due (literally heave-offering). This heave-offering implies the elevation and sanctification of the material world. If man performes his task in the world in the same manner as that of the priest, the material world will be elevated to its, rightful place and the ultimate redemption will be achieved.

The story about the sages is the only real narration in the *Haggadah*. It is evident that this story is told in order to illustrate how the *Seder* observance should be conducted. Further, the *Haggadah* continues with a long drawn-out answer to the four questions in which the events of the Exodus are discussed and the Divine Being is extolled.

Something which resembles a narration and which is in any case, almost a separate entity is the observation that there are four sons, a wise son, a wicked son, a stupid or simple son and a son who does not even know how to ask questions. With the exception of the latter, each son asks about Passover. The *Haggadah* then gives a suitable answer for each son. Only the wicked son, who asks about the purpose of the whole ritual in a manner which indicates that he wishes to exclude himself from it, receives the answer that had he been in Egypt he would not have been liberated. On the other hand, the son who, as yet, is unable to ask any questions has to be told about the Exodus in such a way that he also becomes involved.

Rabbi Schneerson explains the "four sons" as referring to four types of people. In these four categories are comprised the whole of the Jewish people, since the text of the *Haggadah* in naming the four types of sons, employs the conjunction 'and' – the wise son, and the wicked son, and etc. Evidently a different approach is necessary for each type in order to arrive at revelation from concealment. The wise son is only wise if he can transform the bad son into a good son, since 'and' creates a connection between the wise and the bad son. The simple son is given a patient answer to his question and the son who does not even know how to ask, and who is therefore unable to take the initiative in order to achieve revelation, has to be helped. In other words, here also the individual is seen as part of a whole. During the ritual one is moved to identify oneself with the collectivity.

The Hebrew expression for the Exodus from Egypt is *yetziat mitzrayim*. Hebrew is usually written only with consonants, and no vowel signs. A word consisting of consonants only can thus be read with another vowel combination thereby changing its meaning. *Yetziat mitzrayim* can be pronounced and read as *yetziat maitzarim* – meaning to go out of, or transcend, one's limitations. Both terms illustrate the twofold meaning of the *Seder* ritual. On the collective level, there is an exodus from exile in order to attain a Messianic redemption. On the level of the individual, there is an exodus from one's limitions as a human being, the personal redemption indicated in the story of the sages. It is significant that the *Haggadah* states that a person's religious obligations with respect to the *Seder* are not fulfilled until he feels himself that he is liberated from Egypt i.e. from his own shortcomings.

These themes are constantly brought to the fore in the *Seder*. Four cups of wine are drunk, which represent, not only the four expressions of redemption but also the four occasions that the Jewish people have been freed from exile: Egypt, Babylon, the Hellenistic occupation of the land of Israel, and the present exile which began with the Roman conquest of Judea. The four periods of exile are also related to the four questions or, on a deeper symbolic level, the four types of concealment. Exile and redemption can be contrasted and categorized as follows:

exile	redemption
night	day
darkness	light
concealment	revelation
death	life
bitter	sweet
diaspora	homeland

It is surely not accidental that the egg which is related to death is located at the left of the *Seder* plate and the bone related to life at the right. Despite the fact that the bitter herbs are placed in the center, it is tempting to place both categories right and left before exile and redemption. This would be to follow Needham (1973), who showed that in many cultures the opposition between right and left plays a central role in this sort of analysis. Furthermore, then, these pairs of opposites can be included in a more general symbolic classification of Jewish culture (see Meijers 1987 and Douglas 1993:115).

The main themes of the *Seder* are the liberation from Egyptian slavery, the exodus which follows and the entry into and taking possession of the homeland: "Next year in Jerusalem". These themes, have their origin in the cultural and historical experience of the Jewish people. In particular the themes "exile", "redemption" and "homeland" have been constantly reiterated for thousands of years under all kinds of social conditions (cf. Gruber Fredman 1983:114; Meijers, 1984). Every year they are experienced anew on the *Seder* night.

The Social Coercion Resulting from a World Network

The huge emotional attachment to the *Seder* ritual which is to be found among the Jews to this day would appear to indicate that the themes emphasized in this ritual have a perennial relevance and topicality. What kind of social conditions cause this continual reliving of particular ideas and values?

This question becomes even more pointed if we remember that the geographic and socio-economic setting of the orthodox-Jewish "religious regimes", to use Bax's term (1987), was in a constant state of flux. What all these "regimes" had in common was their special status in society. Jews have almost always, and in almost every place, been placed in a marginal and isolated position. As migrants without landed property, but with business interests which extended beyond national borders, practicing their own separate religion and as economic competitors with other social strata they belonged neither to the one nor to the other social class. As a consequence of economic and political developments in Eastern and Central Europe the power struggle between the differing political and religious groups eventually led to the total exclusion of the Jews. The authorities in various places tolerated their presence only in so far as they could profit from the financial advantage of the Jews' international business connections (Meijers 1989:17). The situation of the Jews of Western Europe differed from that of their brethren in Eastern Europe, due to the fact that the majority of Western European Jews had fled eastwards in the Middle Ages. In spite of this, they were officially treated as a minority group at least until after the French Revolution but in practice for a much longer period.

The position of the Jews in the Ottoman Empire was very similar. Although their situation was in general more favorable than in Christian Europe, the Islamic monarchs considered them to be third-class citizens. In no country were they equal to the other citizens. Everywhere, they acted as mediators between the different social classes, they became brokers, forming a buffer between two or more social strata and continously holding what Weber called a "pariah-position" (Weber 1960:3). The lower classes always felt that they were being exploited by the Jews because of the professional services the latter performed for the higher classes. At the same time, as many professions were closed for them, their social situation forced them to perform these services in exchange for income and protection. Through being favored by one class, they attracted the hatred of the other class. In general, the situation of the Jews was the result of a complex interplay between different social forces in societies in which they were strangers. Because of their special status they were constantly oppressed and persecuted. It was therefore a psychological and a social necessity to form a closely-knit group that would be easily recognizable for refugees from other Jewish communities. In fact, this was one of the principal features of a Jewish community: its members were constantly aware that they might have to appeal to each other for assistance. In this way an extensive world-wide "support-network" developed.

The strength of this global network, dependent as Jews everywhere were on external, social factors, was often uncertain. At any event, in their own local communities Jews exerted great pressure on each other to conform to their own norms, and values. This internal pressure resulted in a personal inner constraint which, in a certain sense, was just as powerful as the external pressure from the host society. Assimilation into the host society in order to avoid the internal pressure was difficult, not to say impossible. It meant severing all previous links and relationships. Moreover, there was so much antagonism to these constantly migrating people, that assimilation was never a real possibility. This was also the case in those countries which were relatively good for the Jews. All too often misfortune struck for no apparent reason. As a result Jews everywhere were apprehensive of any social unrest or tension. This was especially true whenever this tension had any connection whatsoever with Jews. This in turn led to an oversensitivity whereby anti-Semitism was perceived in situations where it did not even exist, a tendency to translate every kind of aggression with which Jews were confronted into anti-Semitic terms. In recent times, this process has been intensified by better means of communication. News of the occurrence of a calamity could be disseminated with greater rapidity. As a result of global networks and the interdependence of the Jewish communities, stresses and strains, sometimes only psychological, did not remain confined to a specific locality. Anxiety and fear could spread from one place to another. The only place of refuge, offering protection and repose, was with one's own kind.

Evidently, the ideas and rituals most cardinal to Judaism would be bound to allude to this problem and moreover would be transmitted almost unchanged from one generation to the next. This was even more true in a situation which could be really called "slavery". In those circumstances the only possibility of mentally surviving was identifying oneself strongly with a collective Jewish identity of a free nation with its own territory.

Conclusion

In contrast to what one might have expected, the notions and values which are apparent in the *Haggadah* are as eloquent today as in former times. The ordeals of the Second World War, the struggle for Israel's existence, and the difficult position of the Jews in many countries constantly confirm the relevance of these ideas. Although there are numerous places where Jews are able to live freely and undisturbed, a glance in the newspaper will indicate that the problem of being Jewish is constantly re-appearing. It does not matter whether the news is about the influence of the Jewish lobby in the United States, the spread of anti-Semitism in Eastern Europe or the situation in Israel. These news reports sometimes produce reactions that are stronger than are necessary from a realistic standpoint. This is especially true regarding the situation in Israel, a country which more than any other is a symbol of the future Messianic redemption from exile as well as being a homeland for the Jewish people. The significance of the *Haggadah* in connection with the establishment of, and settlement in the Jewish homeland is even greater now that the future of the territories which have been in Israeli hands since the wars of 1967 and 1973 is under international pressure. In order to understand Jewish feelings concerning this area, it is important to realize that it is not a question of political imperialism, but of fundamental values which are at stake here. The heated emotions connected with this issue are a fundamental part of a Jewish cultural and historical identity which developed in the course of many hundreds of years. Because of the marginal position of the Jews everywhere in the world during the whole of this period, this identity is constantly being re-confirmed and strengthened. And this identity is re-affirmed annually in the *Haggadah*.

Notes

1. I am grateful to Mart Bax and Peter Kloos who commented on an earlier version of this paper.
2. It may be this shared notion of the importance of the festival, which for the Christian emphasizes Christ's last meal and for the Jew the Exodus from Egypt, both major religious facts, that lies behind why throughout history it was precisely during *Pesach* that Jews were so often accused of ritually murdering Christian children and using their blood for baking the unleavened bread necessary for the *Seder*.
3. According to the orthodox journal *Hamachane Hachareadi* (d.d. 24.3 1983 p. 1) 80% of Israel's population observed most of the rather complex religious laws of *Pesach*.
4. This information is based on an interview with a survivor.
5. The various meanings of the ritual are found in the *Haggadah shel Pesach nusach Lubavitch* which is here mainly used for explanation.

References

Bax, Mart 1987: Religious regimes and state formation: towards a research perspective. In: *Anthropological Quarterly* 60 (1): 1–11.

Douglas, Mary 1993: *In the wilderness. The doctrine of defilement in the Book of Numbers.* Sheffield.

Dubnow, Simon 1927: *Weltgeschichte des Jüdischen Volkes.* Band VI. Berlin.

Gilbert, Martin 1985: *The Jews of hope. The plight of Soviet Jewry today.* Harmondsworth.

Gruber Fredman, Ruth 1983: *The Passover Seder.* New York.

Haggadah shel Pesach (according to the Lubavitch liturgy).

Meijers, Daniel 1984: 'Civil religion' or 'civil war'? – Religion in Israel. In: Eric R. Wolf, ed.: *Religion, power and protest in local communities. The Northern shore of the Mediterranean*, pp. 137–161. Berlin.

Meijers, Daniel 1987: The structure of the Jewish calendar and its political implications. In: *Anthropos* 82 (4/6): 603–610.

Meijers, Daniel 1989: *De revolutie der vromen. Ontstaan en ontwikkeling van het chassidisme. Waarin is opgenomen het verslag van reb Dan Isj-Toms reis door de eeuwigheid.* Hilversum.

Needham, Rodney ed. 1973: *Right & Left. Essays on dual symbolic classification.* Foreword by E.E. Evans-Pritchard. Chicago and London.

Schneerson, Rabbi M.M. 1962: *Likutei Sichois.* Vol. II. Brooklyn, N.Y.

Turner, Victor W. 1969: *The ritual process. Structure and anti-structure.* London.

Weber, Max 1960: *Ancient Judaism.* Translated and edited by Hans H. Gerth and Don Martindale. Glencoe (Ill).

Political Protest and Snobbery

Fashion among Cracow Students in the Early 1950s

Leszek Dzięgiel

Dzięgiel, Leszek 1997: Political Protest and Snobbery. Fashion among Cracow Students in the Early 1950s. – Ethnologia Europaea 27: 67–77.

The ethnological research on the everyday life of big Polish cities has only commenced. The author describes a series of customary behaviours connected with the dress of the students of Cracow in the years 1945–1956. Basing on the newspapers of those times and on his own memories, the author discusses the fashion of that period, the ways of obtaining the clothing and its alteration necessary since a considerable part of it came from the military stores of the Western armies. A proper haircut and a special way of bearing were chosen to match the dress. It was a demonstration in opposition to the uniform propagated by the Communist youth organisation, a manifestation of the philosophy of life. According to the author that fashion was a conscious form of the protest expressed by the academic youth against the cultural unification introduced by the totalitarian system formed in Poland in the period following World War II.

Professor dr Leszek Dzięgel, Director, Instytut etnologii, Uniwersytetu Jagiellońskiego, ul. Grodzka 52, PL–31-044 Kraków, Poland. E-mail: dziegiel@grodzki.phils.uj.edu.pl

For centuries the student community has been an essential component of Cracow's cultural environment. The life and customs of old-time students have often provided a rewarding field of exploration for novelists, poets, playwrights and scholars. The last-mentioned group has been exhibiting a particularly keen interest in the distant past, which has acquired a nostalgic patina of centuries gone by (Stepanova 1996:82–93), undergoing an ever increasing mythologization and distortion in the process. On the other hand, everyday life and popular customs in more recent times have received much less scholarly attention, even though a lot of written sources and iconographic materials are available, to say nothing of the remembrances of people who began studies in Cracow less than half a century ago. Ethnological and anthropological reflection on the everyday life of big cities in Poland in the 20th century is still at the beginning stage. Scholars who deal with those matters have often relied so far on the popular-culture model and concentrated on the analysis of various manifestations of so-called "plebeian customs". This is certainly the case in Cracow, where the favourite topics include the annual Emaus fairs at Easter, the antics of Lajkonik (a man dressed up as a Tartar rider during a popular festival in summer), solemn religious processions, parades of craftsmen's guilds etc. Some attention has also been given to the city's market places, particularly in connection with the contacts between Cracow and the neighbouring villages. Incidentally, the suburban village has sometimes offered a convenient and "safe" subject of research for an ethnologist venturing for the first time into the domain of "urban anthropology".

The life of students and the young generation of educated people in present-day Cracow is usually viewed in an artistic or hedonistic perspective (Godula (ed.) 1995:239–290). Other aspects of everyday life have usually been absent from the literature, or at least from publications about Cracow.

The late 1940s and the first half of the 1950s present a particularly interesting period for a historian of Polish culture or an ethnologist, in view of the political circumstances of those days. The programmes of forced "re-education" of society took particularly drastic forms in big cities, such as Cracow, Warsaw or Poznań. The generation of adolescents and young adults, being a category traditionally opposed to all forms of pressure and any attempts to impose by decree uniform patterns of daily life, reacted by specific forms of protest, escapism and rejection of the officially approved way of life. Under the peculiar circumstances of Stalinist Poland, this protest against ideologically determined, forced uniformity did not lead to pluralism in preferences and tastes. At least in the field of popular fashion and entertainment it gave rise to a more or less uniform type of popular culture, which was simply the negation of the model officially professed by the simple-minded social engineers. The ideological war in the field of popular culture in post-war Poland that the communist system waged against society and lost constitutes an extensive area of exploration for students of customs, not only in Poland, but in entire Central and Eastern Europe. So far, however, this area has been sadly neglected (Dzięgiel 1995).

Issues of fashion, clothes, entertainment and resistance to ideological pressure in daily life were dealt with by Leopold Tyrmand (who died in the United States a couple of years ago) in his columns, novels and essays (Tyrmand 1955, 1980). We owe him at least some fairly adequate accounts of cultural situations. His observations, however, were usually made from the point of view of well-to-do or even elitist circles of Warsaw of the 1950s and the Warsaw underworld, linked with that first group by various kinds of dealings. Tyrmand's position in Warsaw society did not exactly place him in close contact with the student circles of Warsaw, with all their social, financial and cultural differentiation. He was, however, one of the few authors fascinated by this aspect of contemporary culture.

The intention of the present essay is simply to acknowledge the existence of a new research area, using as an example the popular student fashion in an old, big-city academic centre. The description of cultural elements presented below results from the author's own experience and observations made during his studies at the Jagellonian University in the years 1950–1955 among a group of fellow students of both sexes. Additional reflection was made possible by the author's field studies in ethnography carried out in those years in various rural regions of Poland.

In the early 1950s, fashion – as well as entertainment – played a principal role in the bizarre war the object of which was to promote an ideologically appropriate lifestyle. Today, after all those years, the official attempts to bring into uniformity the fashion of trousers or skirts may seem ridiculous – reminiscent of those rare instances of crazy regimes where ideological totalitarianism still reigns supreme. One might wonder how the dogmatic official propagandists could fail to see the futility of their fierce and frenzied attacks. Back then, however, things looked different.

For many people, the defence of their individual tastes in the field of clothing became a surrogate battlefield where they fought for their right to privacy and to individual preferences. It was a struggle for personal liberty.

Unimportant and trivial issues of hairstyle and clothing were often blown up out of all proportion. It was a strategy of the system to provoke hysteria over matters of no consequence. When, many years later, the system itself resigned from some of its ideological incantations and symbols, it left behind an often idolatrous cult of the very lifestyle it had vainly tried to eradicate. The artificially maintained isolation of millions of young people from everyday elements of the Western civilization left society in a state of infantilism. One of its manifestations was the attitude of young Poles – but also Czechs, Slovaks, Hungarians or Russians – towards modern fashion. The ideological war of the early 1950s in the field of entertainment and fashion has long since ended, but until now it remains an area where reactions of society are devoid of all criticism and objective reflection. This is highly typical of civilizationally retarded neophytes who have lived in a state of cultural isolation.

Jazz, chewing gum, Coca-Cola – these were the symbols of the alleged corruption of the non-communist world and at the same time elements of an extremely naively construed mythology of the West. Having banned Western novelties, the regime forfeited the chance to gain popularity even among the most primitive groups of the youth, whose support it tried to win in the first place. The officially extolled drabness would soon lose any appeal, while things attacked by the state propaganda as manifestations of bourgeois, Western tastes were promoted to the rank of forbidden fruit. In some young people, however, the authorities managed to reinforce complexes and the sense of powerlessness. Those people had come to believe that stagnation, drabness and banality constituted a virtue. They let themselves be persuaded that novelty and change in everyday life signified an attempt to destroy their world.

The East, on the other hand, had little to offer that could really impress the thousands of young people who yearned for civilizational advancement. What made things even worse, post-war Poland, deliberately impoverished and reduced to the status of a cultural backwater, had likewise ceased to appeal to the greater part of the youth in the long run, despite the noisy propaganda. This was also the case with clothing, which usually plays a very important role in the life of young people of both sexes, as a means of expressing one's personality, aspirations, expectations and sense of membership of the group which one accepts.

The offer of the state-owned shops was out of fashion and in poor taste, both in terms of design and colours. Ladies' garments could make even the most beautiful girl look ugly. The shapeless coats and jackets, heavily padded at the shoulders, gave everyone a squat look. The shoulder padding was seen in those years as an epitomy of conservatism and bad taste. Awkward, mass-produced dresses were neither short, nor long, neither loose, nor tight, and had a lot of pretentious frills around the neckline. Women's footwear imitated the kitschy designs of the late 1930s. Only private boutiques, whose number dwindled rapidly, would offer a limited selection of stylish fashions at exorbitant prices.

Looking back today, nearly half a century later, at the official fashion and goods sold in state-owned shops in those times, one can see that it was an impoverished and vulgarized variety of the type of clothing worn in the years 1939–1940 (Dziekońska-Kozłowska 1964:271–296).

Modern fashion would reach the cordoned-off Poland of the 1950s slowly and selectively. The so-called "new look", which marked the reaction of the West against the wartime restrictions and military requirements that even women had had to comply with, came to Poland only much later, half-heartedly and, occasionally, in highly distorted forms (Dziekońska-Kozłowska 1964:297–356). The witty, illustrated guide to modern dress by Barbara Hoff and Jan Kamyczek, *Jak oni się mają ubierać* [The way they should dress] had yet to appear, in the wake of the fundamental political and ideological changes of 1956 (Hoff & Kamyczek:1956). Meanwhile, inspiration had to be derived from Western films, shown in ever decreasing numbers, and sometimes from old copies of Western magazines. This unnatural isolation left the young generation with a nearly pathological craving for novelties, ideas or gimmicks of all kinds originating from the mythical land of well-being, where life was supposed to run smoothly and colourfully to the rhythmical sound of music. And in the Stalinist era no one would make the young generation any promises of a "speedy accession to Europe"! On the contrary, society was told daily that very soon the revolutionary anger of the masses was going to erupt, plunging the rest of the world in the drab reality. On hearing this, many a young man would think that if the worst came to the worst, it would nevertheless be nicer to be on the other side of the Iron Curtain when that mythical revolutionary eruption took place... Or, meanwhile, to get to a place where one could at least enjoy the material goods denied to the people at home.

As in the case of women's fashion, also men's wear showed the same boring styles in every shop selling factory-made clothes. Likewise, an air of dead seriousness emanated from the official photographs of the highest-ranking dignitaries. I remember a visit of a group of Soviet experts on power industry, after which the baggy, awkward-looking double-breasted jackets they wore received the epithet "high-powered" in student parlance. Decades would have to pass before party activists started to read fashion magazines, use the services of beauticians and masseuses, or play tennis in order to get slim. In the 1950s, men's fashion promoted by the official elite reflected the tastes from the first years of World War II. This becomes quite apparent when one confronts it with old American films or with archive photographs taken at conferences and meetings of statesmen from the East and the West.

Navy blue or dark brown double-breasted pinstripe suits were popular with people of unrefined taste, be they rich or poor. Men wore oversized jackets stiff with padding at the shoulders, with very narrow lapels. Trousers creased at the waistband with numerous seamings. A factory-made shirt could be recognized at a mile's distance by its pale hue and pointed collar.

The conformist's neck was adorned by a narrow tie, the shape and design of which brought to mind its pre-war antecedent. Anyway, it differed radically from the broad, florid fashions popular in the West, whose appearance in Poland was in a way the first sign of protest against the officially accepted style in clothing.

In warmer seasons, people usually wore greenish canvas coats with side pockets and a belt, called "Canadians", although they had nothing to do with Canada. In winter these were replaced by homespun coats of a similar design, usually herringbone patterned. Some people, though not many, still preferred the "partisan" style, with breeches and long boots (so-called "officer boots"). Hats were rare among students. In contrast, clerks and, generally, persons of rank enjoyed wearing their "felts". The young generation, on the other hand, often wore homespun caps. City hoodlums would often stuff newspaper underneath for elegance; this type of headgear earned the nickname "thug caps", first used by Warsaw newspapers and then adopted in Cracow. In winter, pre-war style ski-caps were still in use.

In the area of footwear, black leather dominated. Brown shoes appeared in shops on a more substantial scale only after the so-called "October transformations". Impecunious students usually wore black shoes or ankle-high laced boots with flat toecaps and leather or rubber soles, ugly and styleless. On hot days, some put on broad-strapped sandals, while others wore tennis shoes, usually of a "dark white" colour. They were restored to their original appearance with the use of chalk, hence chalk marks were not an infrequent sight on the pavements.

The first livelier addition to the otherwise drab and shapeless attire of a student from the country who had just enrolled at the university could have been a peaked velvet cap the colour of which symbolized the particular faculty of the university, or an angular, cream-coloured *rogatywka* cap (the traditional design worn by the Polish army). Officials from the party and the ZMP youth organization viewed those kinds of headgear with suspicion, as alleged "relics of the bourgeois and corporatist past" ("corporations" were pre-war student societies). But the favourite among young men on the threshold of adulthood was a black, felt beret. Being of poor quality, it quickly lost shape in the rain and bulged like a mushroom cap. It was said that young men in black berets sometimes fell victim to the aggression of street gangs, hostile to students. I cannot say how true these rumours were.

A student freshly admitted to the university would usually shun carrying his notes and textbooks in a briefcase: that would have been too much like at school or in an office. Instead, he would go to a "sports shop" (which was not exactly what we would expect it to be today ...) and buy a shoulder bag of yellow leather. Students who did some fieldwork particularly favoured those quasi-military-style bags, in addition to which they often put on in winter a brown "aviator's cap" made of artificial leather. The same kind of headgear was also used by official functionaries dispatched to the countryside to perform their duties, and, of course, by motorcyclists. Crash helmets were not yet mandatory in those days. For us, the clerks from the revenue board or the PZU insurance company wrapped up in their trench coats, speeding by on their company-owned motorcycles on the way to the countryside, briefcases dangling from their shoulders on a narrow strap – or returning home in a state of utter exhaustion –

made delightful figures of fun.

Students of the Academy of the Fine Arts and of the faculty of architecture at the Technical University proudly carried around their huge sketch pads or cardboard tubes for tracing paper. It was a matter of nobilitation and chick for them. Malicious tongues would say, however, that the very fact of showing off one's sketch pad did not necessarily amount to much: after all even pre-war maidservants had been known to dress up as secondary school students!

In winter, the sports fashion that the poor young man from the country could afford was a pair of pipe-legged skiing trousers let into old-fashioned skiing boots with straps covering the laces. In this outfit he would trudge boldly through the puddles in Cracow's Main Market Place, even though he had never in his lifetime gone skiing. He neither knew how to, nor could afford it. A true skiing snob from the slopes of Kasprowy Wierch would no longer dare to show up in the Tatra Mountains dressed like that. Also weekend tourists and mountaineers observed their own dress codes in order to express their aspirations and emphasize their participation in particular youth groups. This issue deserves a more extensive treatment (Dzięgiel 1994).

Whenever the everyday style of dress worn by young people in the early 1950s went beyond the most primitive and banal patterns proposed by the clothes stores, it began to reflect the yearnings, aspirations, petty triumphs, and frustrations of the generation. Simultaneously, it opened up – inevitably – the way for various, often ridiculous forms of affectation and snobbery.

The war had ended only five years before. The shabby victors from the East made themselves seen everywhere, and yet the myth of the other victorious army was still alive: the army whose arrival from the West and from across the ocean had been awaited for so many years. An efficient, elegant and at the same time friendly army, which for reasons best known to itself had stopped somewhere halfway across occupied Germany and remained immobile, leaving us to become prey to primitive barbarians. In that period of frustrated expectations and lingering hopes, the demand for clothing from American military stores acquired first of all a symbolic dimension. Aesthetic considerations played a secondary role here and practical utility was the least important (Kantor 1982).

Interestingly enough, in the same years Polish peasants set a high value on items of clothing used by the Polish People's Army. On the weekly market in the town of Nowy Targ, uniforms with buttons covered with olive-coloured fabric and fatigue caps of the *rogatywka* type were lined up on the stalls, invariably attracting crowds of buyers. Fashion dictated that a young farmhand or shepherd should be wearing a khaki jacket, nonchalantly unbuttoned to reveal underneath a home-knit sweater of coarse wool, adorned with silhouettes of deer. Other attributes of the highland dandy included a *rogatywka* cap, boisterously tilted backwards and homespun trousers (*portki*) adorned in front with an ornate embroidered pattern (*parzenice*), let into ankle-high rubber boots of the kind used for spreading manure. By contrast, Cracow students of those days, who had to undergo mandatory military training at the university, did not think much of the style of the uniforms of their commanding officers, to say nothing of the faded dungarees they had to wear in the field, which were an object of constant ridicule.

Thus in big-city market-places, the Polish People's Army outfit occupied only a marginal position, unlike Western military garments.

Clothes of the latter type were much sought after for many years after the war, despite their high prices and signs of wear and tear. Jackets with frayed collars, patched battle-dress blouses or windbreakers with greasy folds had their dedicated fans who painstakingly washed, cleaned and repaired them. In those years, filth, tatters, rags and studied sloppiness were not yet in fashion. What did matter was the design and the unequalled touch of the types of fabrics invented by the leading British and American military labs. Buyers paid attention to colour, but the main thing was the comfortable and clever design of every article of military clothing produced overseas.

The greater part of those garments came from Britain, brought to Poland by former Polish soldiers returning home from the West. For many years they could be seen wearing old, sand-coloured battle-dress and black berets. Sometimes they might sell you a worn-out, tight-fitting military overcoat made of cloth or a neat, brown trench-coat of the type called – nobody knew why – "Major Belt coat". Despite the wear and the passing of years, they were particularly elegant.

Even better-fitting, however, were American military clothes. Comparing the outfit of the two armies, one would notice the British inability to combine chic with comfort and functionality in the design of special-purpose garments. British military boots, for instance, were extremely comfortable and offered ideal protection against water. But their colour and shape left much to be desired and sometimes provoked scorn. It was not so with the American outfit. Likewise, the short British battle-dress blouses that could be cleverly fastened to the trousers did not prove functional for civilian use. The American olive-coloured, hip-length uniform blouses, on the other hand, were more comfortable. Among the many different jackets from the U.S., the veritable legend of those times was the lightweight canvas type with a woollen lining, of the kind worn by General Patton. It was also in those times that the first four-pocketed blouses with a waistband made their appearance. After the Korean War they were adopted by most armies of the world, except in the Communist block. In winter, the brown airmen's sheepskin coats, narrow at the hips and fitted with big collars, sold for outrageous prices.

Another big hit with young dandies was military trousers: tight-fitting, made of sand-coloured cotton. An appropriate complement to these was a dark olive-coloured pullover. Some, though not many, would don in addition a close fitting canvas cap with a large, square peak. It was either turned upwards, in the style favoured by the heroes of wartime films about crews of the B-17 Flying Fortresses, or tilted down so as to screen the forehead and eyes. Dark, rectangular sunglasses à la General MacArthur were also a much coveted object that most people could only dream of.

In wintertime, military fashion enthusiasts hunted not only for the aforementioned airforce sheepskin coats, but also for the popular navy-type duffel coats. In this way the outfit worn by the seamen of the allied forces sailing across the icy waters of the North Sea or Atlantic had become a status symbol for those Poles who could afford it. Many years later, the hooded coat became so popular that even state-owned manufacturers started to turn out garments of a similar fashion, although of a much poorer quality. The design thus became commonplace and finally went out of fashion.

The attraction of the military outfit was its 100-per-cent authenticity. That was the real thing, not an imitation suited to the liking of the youngsters of the kind you can see in "army shops" today. Back then, no one would have thought of wearing colourful badges of imaginary units or an admiral's epaulets.

The type of clothing I am writing about was available, although in a very narrow selection, from second-hand commission-sale shops, so called *komisy,* which charged ridiculous prices. Those who ventured to market places in small towns had a chance to get Western clothes at a fraction of that cost. This was particularly true about regions from which the most peasants had once emigrated to America as, for instance, the Carpathians, but also the Kurpie region in northern Poland. Descendants of the one-time village paupers whom hunger had driven to America now showered their Polish relatives with hand-me-downs. Overseas fashion did not suit the local, provincial tastes. Thus clothes one could see in a fashion magazine were often used around the house or farm for the dirtiest chores. We often observed, much to our horror, good-natured farmers digging potatoes or spreading manure dressed in rags that had once been the most elegant suits or jackets. More and more often, however, pedlars would call at peasants' cottages: the Western clothes they would buy there dirt cheap could be resold in town at a huge profit. Some of those salesmen were regular visitors at student hostels, always carrying a bag of attractive merchandise. They were eagerly awaited by their regular customers. Others, however, went straight to the market place.

For several decades, Cracow's flea market, called *tandeta* in the local idiom, was constantly being relocated from one place in the outskirts of the town to another. The communist authorities had hoped it would wither away; it grew, instead, out of all proportions. The funny thing is it keeps expanding now, in the wake of the stormy political transformations going on in Central and Eastern Europe. A whole new type of small private shops selling second-hand clothes of Western origin has sprung up. They are popularly called "*lumpexy*" – an ironic reference to the Pewex network of stores that until 1990 sold luxury goods for hard currencies, and to the Lumpenproletariat, the alleged clientele of those new shops, who buy such luxuries as they can afford. In the times I am writing about no such shops existed. The commission-sale second-hand shops – *komisy* – were of an entirely different character.

In the early 1950s, Cracow's main *tandeta* was situated in the Podgórze borough: off Kalwaryjska street, not far from present-day Krasickiego-Boczna street. All the buyers and sellers were Polish. The only slightly more exotic ethnic element was a very small group of local Gypsies. Twice a week, the trams bound for Podgórze were bursting at the seams in the morning hours. Riding to the *tandeta* were all kinds of strange and dubious characters. It was rumoured that the city authorities, hostile to the bazaar and to anything that did not fit into the economic patterns imposed upon the city, deliberately took some trams off the route on those days. I don't know whether that was really the case. Anyway, experienced bazaar-goers would remind you to take good care of your wallet in the cramped vehicle rolling down Kalwaryjska street.

A muddy path led from the shabby and ugly street to an enclosure surrounded partly by a wall and partly by a fence. At the entrance swarmed groups of individuals of both sexes, dressed in drab clothes, who were trying to dupe the newcomers into a deal. They would offer to buy goods brought by others – at ridiculously low prices – only to try to sell the same thing at a profit a couple of metres away. *Tandeta* regulars treated those petty tricksters with a haughty indifference. They steered carefully, clothes-filled bags in hand, among the rows of sellers proffering their wares. Usually, they did not feel like mixing with that marketplace proletariat, although they did look around to see what was being sold and for how much. Finally, they would make their way to the central part of the *tandeta,* where displayed on tarpaulin sheets lying on the ground (plastic was not used for such purposes in those times: it was too scarce and precious) were heaps of clothes of foreign origin, guarded by the tradesmen. Depending on the season, those people would stamp about to keep off either the cold, or the boredom. Their faces had become roughened after the hundreds of days spent in the heat or frost. Cigarettes in their mouths, they would smile ingratiatingly at you, displaying yellow teeth. In winter, they would put on – over all the other warm clothes – an additional green or once-white raincoat, so greasy with dirt that every fold of it shone. Women wrapped kerchiefs or shawls – draped turban – like as had been fashionable in the wartime years – around their heads. Experienced buyers would nonchalantly examine the piles of clothes lying on the sheets and ask about the prices with an ostentatious disgust. People who regularly frequented the market place in order to convert goods received from the West into cash were often well known among the *tandeta* elites. Every so often someone would accost them to inquire about the contents of the bags they carried. It was typical for such a seller to have a close circle of regular buyers. Some customers, however, were best avoided as potential informers.

To the left, next to the wall, there operated sellers of the worst kind of rags and totally worn-out shoes. Those items, offered for sale for a song, had often been extracted from the spacious wardrobes of old Cracow flats, for the purpose of being thrown away. All kinds of goods found buyers in that section of the *tandeta,* but then the amounts of money that changed hands in the process were negligible. Shoes and boots that were worn-out beyond repair were often bought by some country shoemaker who would use them as material for mending other shoes, or, alternatively, would patch them up somehow and sell them to a village beggar. Such was the condition of the merchandise that some prospective clients were inclined to poke about it with a stick. On the other hand, the interest aroused by this section of the *tandeta* speaks volumes about the economic situation of the Poland in those years. No owner of a "lumpex" shop in Cracow, selling used clothes by the kilogram, would dare to include this kind of stuff in his offer.

The Cracow *tandeta,* like all public gatherings, must have been routinely observed by the secret police. However, the number of pickpockets operating there no doubt exceeded the number of informers.

Most students visited the *tandeta* for social rather then mercantile reasons. Their miserable scholarships would hardly allow them to buy things there, even though many an item of clothing aroused an unbearable desire. And yet the style-conscious youngsters were regular visitors in Kalwaryjska street, if only to keep abreast of the latest fashions. For many years it was a fitting thing to do to boast about some supposedly excellent bargain one had made at the *tandeta*. Nobody, even the swankiest person of either sex, felt embarrassed about wearing second-hand and often well-worn clothes, which nevertheless conjured the magic of overseas fashion. It was not just a matter of design. People were fascinated also by the touch of the fabrics, their softness, smoothness and strength. Those clothes felt astonishingly light to wear. The earliest synthetics rustled seductively and no matter how hard you crumpled them, they would return to shape in a second all by themselves, as if by magic. Many years had to pass before the impecunious neophytes of plastic modernity rediscovered the true merits of the despised natural fibres. *Komis* shops with second-hand goods prospered, bazaars expanded. All the while the sorry products of the domestic industry were held in utter contempt. Girls were particularly disgusted with those of their friends who apprehensively altered clothes sent to them from abroad to make them match the traditional, "quiet" designs.

Apart from military outfit, whose flow into Poland had by now shrunk to a trickle, more and more civilian clothes began to reach the market and became the decisive influence on the avant-garde of the early 1950s. It is not true that the most widely followed style in those days was that of *dżolersi*, that is, "jolly boys", whom the official propaganda soon dubbed *bikiniarze*, or "*bikinniks*". A "bikinnik" wore rather shortish trousers, so tight-fitting that they almost required a shoehorn to put on, striped socks and extremely thick-soled shoes. Other attributes included a broad, florid tie, a jacket with padded shoulders but narrow in the waist, and a very broad-brimmed hat with a small crown, called a "pancake hat". A "bikinnik's" hair would be carefully swept back so as to form a so-called "pleureuse" covering his neck. But in the days I am writing about that kind of fashion was popular mostly with Cracow's underworld – the "street-corner society" in which students had no intention to be included. In Western Europe, that rather decadent style had had its followers – thuggish dandies called *zazou* – already during the war and it must have been there and then that Leopold Tyrmand picked up his extravagant style, which shocked his Polish friends so much in the late 1940s (Szarota 1995:81–86, Fig. 28 and 29).

How, then, should a young citizen of Cracow have chosen his clothes and hairstyle in 1951, that is, assuming that apart from the desire to look good, he had access to gift parcels from abroad or, alternatively, enough cash to visit the *tandeta* and the *komis* shops for other purposes than purely cognitive?

First of all, he should have chosen a well-fitted, soft, single-breasted jacket with relatively short but wide lapels, unpadded on the shoulders. Such jackets had, apart from the regular flap pockets, also an additional small pocket at the waist, on the left-hand side – a freak of fashion from a far-off land. Trousers, in their turn, which never had any tucks, had to fit tightly at the hips and then the legs narrowed down, to reach a width of some 20–23 cm at the bottom. They either had a 3-to-4-cm cuff or no cuff at all – that was a hallmark of elegant design. Yet another was the presence of two pockets at the back. Short, pipe-legged, "jolly-boy-style" trousers were left to hooligans to wear – and to official cartoonists to portray in their attempts, as fierce as they were futile, to eradicate the "bikinnik" subculture. Shirt collars had to be small and narrow. Ties had broad fronts and a newly devised, heart-shaped knot had come into fashion. Vulgar images – of the kind of a nude Hawaiian girl under a palm tree – were no longer the vogue.

Light suede shoes on thick rubber soles began to give way to brown and yellow moccasins, which you could easily jump into and out of. Shoes on corrugated soles of thick, hard rubber (popularly called "tractor shoes"), so popular in the subsequent years, had not made their appearance yet.

In view of Cracow's poor climate, an elegant inhabitant of that town would often wear a soft, black beret which admirably withstood rain, unlike its predecessor made of felt. Boys and girls were desperately trying to find one, but private manufacturers somehow could not keep up with the demand, while the giant state-owned producers stuck to the old fashions and ways. When the inexorable Central European frost set in, those who did not shun some eccentricity put on small, woollen caps from military stocks or shapeless commando-style headgear fashioned from double-layered, army-issue scarves. The most stylish thing to do, however, was to go about bareheaded for as long as it was possible.

Girls doing artistic or quasi-artistic studies – particularly if they were well-off – were more ambitious, as far as clothing was concerned, than ones from other milieux and schools. They preferred sports clothes of Western origin. On their heads, they usually wore red headscarves, imprinted with a pattern and bearing a "FAST COLORED" notice; these could also be used as neckerchiefs. Their clothes were colourful, unpretentious – and expensive. On cold days, it was fashionable to wear bright yellow three-quarter coats of camel wool or ladies' duffel coats. In 1950, if not earlier, the long-lasting craze began for bright-coloured, striped synthetic sweaters and enormous, colourful nylon kerchiefs which could be worn on the head or tied around the neck. Yet another item which gained great popularity was the zip fastener. It was used everywhere, whether it was necessary or not. Some circles of the Cracow intelligentsia had a penchant for broad, chequered skirts, tight, black, synthetic sweaters and hunter's shoulder bags of yellow leather. This kind of fashion was sometimes perceived as a nostalgic form of protest against the evil times and it endured for many years. Embroidered sheepskin coats of a pre-war design, taken in at the waist, combined with fur caps, were characteristic of the circles of "former landowners", genuine ones and others.

One could not afford to buy fashionable clothes only in expensive *komis* shops or at the nearly equally expensive *tandeta.* People tried to sew their garments themselves or commissioned tailors to do the job. This was made easier by the fact that the early 1950s saw the comeback of a once popular and commonplace type of fabric: corduroy. Initially, people used the standard variety, available in the state-owned stores. Soon, however, the arbiters of fashion declared it banal and ugly. The vogue now was delicate, fine-textured corduroy. It was used first of all for trousers. To be sure, it quickly bulged at the knees and trouser legs were becoming short and baggy. At the folds on the back it crumbled hopelessly, leaving large bald patches. But it was fashionable.

As I said before, trousers had to be well fitted at the hips and back. Today, with all kinds of baggies being in, one finds it hard to believe. In the 1950s, however, people exchanged, with a glint in the eye, addresses of tailors who would undertake to sew trousers of such a design, or, better still, alter an old pair. It was not easy. The Cracow craftsmen of the early 1950s simply could not adjust to the new demands. Usually they refused to do things the way their young clients wished. "What outdated fashions they've got there in America," marvelled a tailor examining a pair of trousers whose design he was supposed to duplicate, borrowed from a friend who had received them in a parcel. Indeed, the new style was reminiscent of the days of Count von Zeppelin's first experiments with airships and the Meyerling tragedy (Banach 1965). Therefore, commissions to alter a pair of trousers or sew a new one usually ended in a miserable failure even of the masters of the art: The tailor had botched the job again! But we were soon to find out that in a narrow passage off the Main Market Place in Cracow there was an "emergency repair shop" run by a truly competent man. He gladly undertook to make all kinds of alterations and even difficult repairs and quickly became our sartorial patron saint of last resort. He never rejected any order, even though its execution was not always perfect. At any rate, among the fashion-conscious students of Cracow, he enjoyed for a while the position of a monopolist.

Gradually, the blue jeans came to be perceived as the best-loved type of trousers of the latter half of the century. In the early 1950s, however, they were only beginning to make their appearance in Poland – creating an unparalleled sensation, both because of the texture of denim, unknown in Poland before, and of their indigo colour (Davis 1992). Their price soon soared to unprecedented levels. Originally, the design and finish of "cowboy trousers" were very traditional. They were lockstitched with a white thread and hardly ever adorned with studs. The first lucky owners proudly rolled up the cuffless legs an inch or two. People were in for another shock when denim jackets arrived. At the bazaar stalls, they were even harder to get and still more expensive.

On warm days, it was fashionable to wear striped synthetic T-shirts, let out loosely over the trousers. This was also the way to wear flannelette sports shirts, which, in accordance with the overseas fashion, should never be tucked in. But what were we to do here, in Central Europe, where shirt buttoning did not usually extend below the waist? Their length was not suited to that fashion, either, as they often ended a little above the knees.

Those who despised the banal pre-war hairstyles while leaving the "pleureuse" to be worn by the shady figures prowling the streets of the Zwierzyniec borough, chose a new type of haircut which was like a crew cut, but longer at the top and sides of the head and shorter at the back. Nowadays you can get this kind of haircut at any barber's shop in Cracow, but in 1950 or 1951 an average hairdresser neither knew nor cared about this style. Fortunately, on the corner of Warszawska and Szlak streets there was a barber who would cut our hair exactly the way we liked. All we had to do was to tell the man at the very outset we wanted our hair cut "weirdo style". He was not an old man yet, but he knew all the tricks of the trade so the customers were always satisfied.

Some female students in those years had their hair cut short with a halo of curls round the face, à la Claudette Colbert. A few girls began to wear their hair tied in a pony tail. Others preferred a permanent wave flowing over the shoulders in the style of Rita Hayworth. In contrast, all kinds of pigtails, buns or plaits running across the shoulder were seen as terribly outdated. On the other hand, hairstyles "à la Fanfan" or "à la Simone" inspired by the new Italian and French cinema were only to appear later.

It is interesting to note that the authorities, so furiously attacking all Western influences in fashion, seemed totally ignorant of the preferences of students and the dress subculture based on *komis* and *tandeta* buys. They invariably assailed the "jolly boy" in a "pancake hat" (Dzięgiel 1993:76–77). The official guards of ideological morality must have thought that clothes received in parcels or purchased at the *tandeta* were worn by poor people who could not afford to buy "decent" dress in normal shops. And a pauper was, in those days, automatically viewed as a worthy, or at least harmless, citizen. Besides, bosses of the ZMP youth organization would sometimes appropriate clothes sent from the West as a gift for the poorest. And as far as hairstyles were concerned, the official propaganda still fought the battle against the "pleureuse" of the "bikinnik", never mind the crew cut. But as a matter of fact, to arouse the least political suspicions, one ought to have been bald.

For decades after World War II, beards or moustache were out of favour with the young generation in Poland. A venerable, old professor might be wearing a moustache, but not a student. Our unforgettable professor of ethnology, for instance, had a grey English moustache à la Clark Gable. Young people were always clean-shaven.

Today the barber's shop at the corner of Warszawska and Szlak streets has given way to a paint shop. The *tandeta* square in Podgórze has long since been built up. Its youthful clientele of the 1950s is approaching retirement.

A separate treatment should be given to the developments in everyday student fashion in the days immediately before the political breakthrough of October 1956. Advocates of traditional- and ZMP-style dress were clearly losing their zeal. The domestic clothing market, weak and inadequate as it was, finally started to imitate Western designs, albeit awkwardly and faint-heartedly. The scanty import of more attractive footwear or clothes from the adjacent countries bred a naive conviction about civilizational advancement of our close neighbours, e.g. Czechoslovakia and Hungary – those mysterious and inaccessible lands which it was only now becoming possible (for the select few) to visit. Nothing, however, could erode the position of the Cracow *tandeta*. For many, many years it was a source of goods that boosted the morale and self-esteem of the frustrated young generation of People's Poland, whom the authorities were trying, with less and less success, to imbue with the only correct ideology.

Translated by Krzysztof Kwaśniewicz

References

Banach, A. 1965: *Portret wzorowego mężczyzny* [A portrait of an exemplary man], Wydawnictwo Literackie, Kraków.

Davis F. 1992: *Fashion, Culture and Identity*, Chicago.

Dziekońska-Kozłowska A. 1964: *Moda kobieca w XX wieku* [Ladies' fashion in the 20th century], Arkady, Warszawa.

Dzięgiel, L. 1993: "Bardziej straszne niż śmieszne" [Rather frightening than funny], *Arka* No. 65(6), Kraków, pp. 64–77.

Dzięgiel, L. 1994: "Wolność reglamentowana" [Rationed freedom], *Universitas* No. 12(4), Kraków, pp. 48–55.

Dzięgiel, L. 1994a: Skok z wybuchem czyli środki pozoracji [Jump with a bang or the art of camouflage], *Kultura* No. 5(560), Paris, pp. 41–59.

Dzięgiel, L. 1995: "Życie codzienne i historia najnowsza – nowe pole badań etnologa" [Everyday life and recent history: A new field of ethnological research], *Universitas PUNO* No. 63, Zürich–London, pp. 7–11.

Godula, R. (ed.) 1995: *Sekrety i klejnoty Krakowa* [The secrets and jewels of Cracow], Wydawnictwo Wawelskie, Kraków.

Hoff, B., and Kamyczek, J. 1956: *Jak oni się mają ubierać* [The way they should dress], Czytelnik, Warszawa.

Kantor, R. 1982: *Ubiór-strój-kostium. Funkcje odzienia w tradycyjnej społeczności wiejskiej w XIX i na początkach XX wieku na obszarze Polski* [Dress-clothes-costume: Functions of clothing in the traditional village community in the 19th and early 20th centuries on the territory of Poland], Uniwersytet Jagielloński, Kraków.

Stepanova I. 1996: Symbolika v odevu prazskych studentu v letach 1848 a 1868 [Symbolism in dresses of Praha students in 1848–1868] In: *Kulturni symboly a etnicke vedomi* (ed.) Jan Pargač, Praha.

Szarota, T. 1995: *Życie codzienne w stolicach okupowanej Europy* [Everyday life in European capitals under Nazi occupation], PiW, Warszawa.

Tyrmand, L. 1955: *Zły* [The evil one], Czytelnik, Warszawa.

Tyrmand, L. 1980: *Dziennik 1954* [Diary: 1954], Polonia Book Fund, Warszawa.

REFLECTING CULTURAL PRACTICE

George E. Marcus, Houston
A Report on Two Initiatives in Experiments With Ethnography a Decade after the „Writing Culture" Critique

Ina-Maria Greverus, Frankfurt
Performing Culture. To Be is Being Spoken With

The Challenge of Field Work

Internationales Symposium zu Ehren von Ina-Maria Greverus

30. - 31. Oktober 1997
Frankfurt a. M.

Carmelo Lisón Tolosana, Madrid
Personal Voices

Hermann Bausinger, Tübingen
Feldforschung am Schreibtisch

Glenn Bowman, Canterbury
Radical Empiricism: Anthropological Field Work after Psychoanalysis and the Année Sociologique

Hans-Peter Köpping, Heidelberg
Bodies in the Field: Sexual Taboos, Self-Revelation and the Limits of Reflexivity in Anthropological Field Work

Christian Giordano, Fribourg
I Can Describe Those Better Whom I Don't Like

Henk Driessen, Nijmegen
The Notion of Friendship in Ethnographic Field Work. A Mediterranean Case Study

Wolfgang Kaschuba, Berlin
Die Feldforschung und die Repräsentation der Ethnologie

Dunja Rihtman-Auguštin, Zagreb
The Ethnoanthropologist in His Native Field: To Observe or to Wittness?

Hans-Rudolf Wicker, Bern
Applied Anthropology, Field Work and the Interaction with Society: The Working and Re-Working of Social Fields

Ulf Hannerz, Stockholm
Of Correspondents and Collages

Massimo Canevacci, Rom
Urban Communication and Polyphonic Representation. Conflicts and Syncretisms in a Comparative Metropolitan Landscape: Sao Paolo, Rome, Berlin

Information und Anmeldung:
Regina Römhild & Cornelia Rohe
Institut für Kulturanthropologie und Europäische Ethnologie
Bettinaplatz 5
D - 63025 Frankfurt a.M.
Tel.: (+49) (0)69 7982 2209
Fax.: (+49 (0)69 7982 8247
e-mail: Roemhild@em.uni-frankfurt.de